Welcoming Food

Diet as Medicine for Home Cooks and Other Healers

Book 1: Energetics of Food and Healing

ANDREW STERMAN

Published by
Classical Wellness Press, New York

ISBN: 978-0-9837720-9-5

The contents of this book are for informational purposes only and are not intended or implied to be a substitute for professional medical advice, diagnosis, or treatment. Always seek the advice of your physician or qualified health provider with any questions you may have regarding a medical condition. Never disregard medical advice or delay seeking it because of something you have read in this or any other book.
If you have a medical emergency, call your doctor, go to an emergency room, or call 911.
References to traditional medicine in this text use the term 'medicine' in a historical context and are not to be understood otherwise. Further, this book may be written in summary, shorthand, or conclusory form and is not to be considered comprehensive. Correspondence with the author does not create a professional relationship and does not create any privacy interests.

Front cover image courtesy of Andrew and Ravi Sterman
Cover and interior design by Cody Dodo

First edition
10 9 8 7 6 5 4 3 2 1

www.welcomingfood.com
Please direct permissions requests to this website.

For Ann, Ravi, and Miriam, who inspire my home cooking
and so very much more.

And in memory of my father, Samuel Sterman,
who taught me to think like a scientist without accepting
the limitations of any one way of mind.

Table of Contents

ONE

Invitation

When we talk about food, we are talking about everything. A good diet nourishes us on all levels—there is no part left out. Our deepest values are encoded within our food choices and traditions; diet is our personal philosophy in action. And while it can get complicated, simple choices make great eating, and that opens the way to positive change. As complex subjects like food begin to reveal their simple truths, that is when they become truly alive, and in this way food takes a new place in our lives—never fussy, but well-informed and filled with good heart.

Diet is a practical way to reach into the myriad elements of our lives. It's earthy, real, and universal. For me, working with food has provided a practice, first as an individual, then as a cook and teacher, as if sharing food were somehow like sharing the benefits of a meditation. My kitchen practice has been evolving for over thirty years, informed by my study of cooking, dietary theory, modern nutrition, and the riches of classical Chinese medical thought.

In these two companion volumes, I am not proposing a specific diet, nor is there judgment on how people live or eat. Rather, here you can learn about the effects of different foods, how to manage good eating from available markets and restaurants, and how to know what works for you and those for whom you cook, all based on time-tested traditional knowledge and appropriate research, with practical details for busy modern living.

I studied cooking technique and wholistic private chef methods in New York, but also gathered a thousand "Here, like this!" lessons through fortuitous meetings on my travels as a concert musician. In Naples, a grandmother-chef took me into her restaurant kitchen to share her traditional way of handling garlic, *pepperoncini*, herbs, vegetables, seafood and meats. In Hong Kong, a friend's mother taught me her own grandmother's way of making congee. On a long flight home from Taipei, a chef in the next seat shared home cooking recipes with me:

Fresh fish with ginger, scallion, rice wine and sesame oil, her family's favorite dinner

Beef noodle stew with herbs for warding off common cold

Tofu with black mushrooms and spices to enhance digestion

Versions of these recipes along with explanations of how they work are included in the second volume, *Welcoming Food: Recipes and Kitchen Practice.*

Beyond the techniques of enthusiastic chefs and home cooks who can't resist sharing their traditions, there is another secret: each food has an intrinsic nature, with influences we can learn to understand. We need to be guided by more than just taste preferences or nutritional analysis. We need to know how different foods affect our internal energetics.

In the Chinese medical classics, diet is not an afterthought or an entertainment, diet is the pinnacle of all medicines. It is a medicine we are all using daily for life support, and if problems arise, it's the first and most important aspect of our lives to adjust. To do this well, a whole new way of thinking is necessary, a flexible mindset capable of making use of the conflicting dietary advice coming at us from all corners. The task is to sort through the many differing viewpoints so that foods can be used as you wish—to make meals more enjoyable, or to embark on a well-informed path of renewal.

I was sensitive to foods as a child—the fact that food choices matter has always been obvious to me. I was "an exception" in modern medicine terms, finding no benefit from a string of well-meaning doctors and their treatments. Gradually I found my way to good health through self-healing with diet, *qigong*, meditation and my chosen art (music). It seemed that I needed to build all my healing tools from scratch; only later did I realize that becoming healthy could be much easier. The purpose of these books is to make rare dietary information openly available and clear, in order to dramatically shorten the time it takes to begin making good use of it.

The tradition of dietary therapy that exists within classical Chinese medicine includes texts nearly two thousand years old and an unbroken oral tradition continually explaining and expanding those texts. I have been extremely fortunate to have received very thorough transmission of this tradition directly from a scholar-practitioner, Dr Jeffrey Yuen, a Daoist master living and teaching in New York City. The nature of that training is unconventional. Teachings are given in precise form, but true understanding (and subsequent application) must be earned on one's own.

To take my food practice to the highest level, I began formal study in Chinese herbal medicine, again with Master Yuen (dietary theory is closely connected to herbal theory). This opened the door to precise diagnostic tools and clinical strategies for tailoring diet for medical conditions (or at the very least to support their treatment) and just as importantly, to cultivate true wellness for those in good health.

All through these years of study and development I've continued to travel extensively as a concert musician. Beyond the profound joys and satisfactions of that, I've been able to gather food secrets in charmingly unlikely encounters. A "heal-all" soup from a cook in Indonesia, an over-eating cure from a chef in Buenos Aires, stay-warm foods from Poland and Russia, and so many treasures from France, Italy, Spain, Japan, Scandinavia, Mexico, China, Turkey, Australia and more. Whatever I learn about cooking, I look at through my training in Chinese medicine dietetics. It's very important to understand that Chinese dietary therapy provides a powerful and clear lens that can be applied to any type of food, from high cuisine to burgers, foods from any continent or tradition. These two volumes are an in-depth introduction to the knowledge needed to understand food and its influences in your own life, using the foods found in any market or wherever you like to eat.

Today, in private sessions, classes for clinicians, and cooking lessons, I work with people whose personal journeys invariably differ from my own, each requiring unique detective work. A quick story.

> A woman came for a consult. She suffered "severe belly pain" daily for more than twenty years. Her doctors had prescribed many things and even conducted an exploratory surgery without finding a cause or achieving resolution. After listening to her story, inquiring about her daily diet, and reading her pulses (a traditional Chinese medicine diagnostic tool), it was clear that she was suffering from *cold* in her stomach exacerbated by too many raw foods, cold drinks and juices. She protested, "But…salads are healthy for you, and juices are super-healthy for you!" Diet is individual, and for her they were causing

a lot of trouble. I recommended that she have all her food cooked and warm (she liked to cook and was pleased at the idea), avoid cold drinks and have vegetable soups instead of vegetable juices. We discussed warming spices such as ginger, scallion, cinnamon, rosemary, oregano, cumin, fennel seed, turmeric, and designed a number of sample meals together. I asked her to stay in touch, but I didn't hear from her after that. Until, that is, about five years later, when she brought her husband for unrelated issues. I gently asked about her own health. "Oh, I'm great! I would have come back, but I didn't need to. I've had no digestive pain since the first day I switched to all warm food. It was a miracle!" The advice was not complicated, but that she followed it impeccably after only one visit was unusual, if not exactly miraculous. Health is always more complex than a simple fix, but she wanted relief from a specific long-standing problem, and without a correction of diet, other treatments could not be successful. Once the detective work was done, the right path became clear. And the patient, honoring her body's specific needs, followed that path to healing.

At some point, we all need to gain real food understanding in a way that makes sense and is workable for us as individuals. Use this book and the companion *Welcoming Food: Recipes and Kitchen Practice* to understand how deeply food engages with all the parts of your life. Most importantly, feel inspired to use the practical tools presented here to gain more joy and freedom in life, first gradually, then fluently and naturally.

Masters and beginners like to keep things simple. Much of the time we feel between the two, but inspired simplicity is always available, and it makes the best meals both for pleasure and for health. Let me try to be simple:

> *Eat what you can digest well and efficiently. Know your personal health. Support the substance of your body while tuning and cultivating your energetic vitality.*

TWO

A Fresh Look at Food

Diet is deeply individual. No two people respond identically to the same foods. Food interactions vary between one person and another, from culture to culture, and as we grow and age. Most importantly, we all respond differently to foods according to our personal health. In order to understand this successfully, we need some knowledge and insight into:

> » The properties of the foods we eat
>
> » The effects of combining foods in different ways
>
> » The cooking methods used
>
> » Our particular health tendencies

Personally, I find all points of view on health interesting. Each has much to offer. However, as modern medicine progresses, increasing specialization makes sensible applications to daily life difficult, particularly in the kitchen. Medical specialists master smaller and smaller pieces of the puzzle, while general advice is never accurate for any individual. Recently, for example, a dietary client reported nausea, insomnia, migraines, and anxiety. She had just been to her doctor who said he could offer a prescription for each symptom, but warned that it would be too much to treat all at once. "Tell me which one is most important, I can treat that, or…you might see a therapist," he'd suggested. Frustrated, she said to me, "All this stuff must be related, I just know it, but I don't know how!"

What we need is a way to tie things together, to connect migraines with nausea, nausea with sleep, emotions with any or all of the above. We can begin by understanding that everything relates to diet and digestion. Even parts of health that seem unrelated can be engaged and tuned through the foods we eat and the ways we cook them. Diet is the centerpiece of all health.

In my search for making the connections between diet and well-being, classical Chinese medicine has provided the most successful approach, being both profoundly intellectual and very effective in practice. The approach of this book is therefore through this lens, while freely integrating ideas and insights from a broad range of modern and classical influences. Why shouldn't we benefit from all that is useful and wise? Modern medicine brings the rigor of laboratory methods while classical medicines bring millennia of insight and experience. If our minds are clear and our hearts open, it's a win-win.

The Scope of Kitchen Dietetics

What if our bodies could talk to us about food, tell us what to choose, what to avoid, which combinations work together, or what dietary factors erode our good health? What if our bodies could say, "Hey, I'm going to have to work all night to digest that kind of dinner!" Or, "Just because your boss was horrible today doesn't mean you have to eat junk food in front of the television all night!" What if our liver could tell us what fried food feels like, or our pancreas could convey how tired it feels after sweets, or our digestion could tell us what it's like with a mash of convenience food inside? What if our glands could express what it's like to be running on caffeine instead of proper food and decent rest? If our bodies could talk to us about food, we might not eat perfectly but at least we'd know better what's going on.

In fact, our bodies *do* speak to us, we just need to learn our inner language. Digestion and the workings of our organs occur under the radar, beneath our normal awareness. We only hear from within when something doesn't feel right, or, in many cases, years down the road when symptoms of an illness "suddenly" appear. The art is to hear the whispers, to learn to tune ourselves as we go, in real time. The results reach to every corner of our lives.

When we say *my liver*, *my pancreas* or *my digestion*, what we really are saying is *me*. More than we think, our organs, glands, bones, muscles, secretions, and all the functions going on inside—they are us and we are that. We could say each organ has a personality, a character, and its own state of well-being. We can know what foods connect to our internal organs, affecting their functions in particular ways. We can know that sweet foods directly stimulate our pancreas and that too much sweet stuff can damage it from overwork. We can know that oils are essential for health, but too much fried food overtaxes our liver. We can learn to hear the inner language of the body, spoken through subtle signs, clear as day once you learn how to listen.

Common sense combined with modern research and the vast traditional wisdom from the dietary branch of Chinese medicine—that is the journey being offered here. This is a tour from appetite through the entire digestive process, in ways that make sense for everyday living with everyday foods. What we need is knowledge we can use. What starts small can change a life, and a single life can initiate a world of change.

In these two companion volumes, I offer a tour of healthy digestion, explanations of what can commonly go wrong, and recipes ranging from comfort foods to therapeutic meals. Each "problem" is accompanied by advice on which foods to avoid and key foods to add. In Book 1: *Understanding Food*, we take a tour of appetite, tasting, chewing, swallowing, digesting, separating, transforming, assimilating, metabolizing, cleansing, and eliminating. Book 2 puts theory into practice with a collection of recipes designed to inspire us to cook, eat well, and further understand the energetics of the dishes we prepare. Because I believe that life is about improvisation and because all diet must be individualized, the recipes are given as templates to be customized (although they also can be followed just as written). Advanced cooking skills are not needed; much of the value of these recipes lies in their simplicity.

By understanding food and being inspired to cook, the home cook can become the director of individual and family health. For many, the ideas in this book represent a new way of thinking. It may take some time to understand true appetizers, how to combine main and side dishes, and to navigate habitual food patterns that make health and happiness elusive. Confidence comes with familiarity and experience. Therefore, occasionally I've taken the opportunity to revisit some important things in different ways. You may find an idea that seems at first to be new or unusual will make common sense when you encounter it later, or when you put it to use in a recipe.

Theory and practice overlap as we shop and cook. For those who rarely (or even never) cook, food knowledge can be applied to ordering food in restaurants and as takeout. Whether a chef, a passionate cook, a "get-it-done" cook, or a non-cook, as new knowledge is supported by personal experience, you won't have to take anyone's word but your own for what is healthy for you.

How to Use This Book

Foods that you eat regularly begin to have a medicinal effect, for better or worse. Seen this way, eating is always an act of self-care. We are doing medicine with ourselves, at all times. This shouldn't make us afraid. Dive in, no fear. Even small dietary improvements will bear fruit.

As for the book itself, treat it like a meal. Eat what you like first, then look around for more. Put it down before you bite off too much at once. Digest well. Some readers may read through in order, others will look for what is of immediate interest—perhaps a favorite food or a particular health issue. Use the index to pinpoint information or read a chapter in full to get the context. Others will start with the recipes and find their way into the theory later. Use it as you wish.

My hope is that a reader will be inspired to make beautiful food that supports health and happiness, individually tailored. And I hope for a lot of questions to be clearly answered.

How Do We Know What We Know?

There are many paths to good knowledge. Well-designed and responsibly conducted modern studies contribute many important details. For example, it's very good to know that pregnant women should have lots of *folate* in their diet and that dark green vegetables such as broccoli, spinach, kale and asparagus offer plenty of it. That's good information and there are many places to find it. Laboratory studies have contributed a great deal to nutrition practice, particularly regarding deficiency illnesses that arise during conditions of relative deprivation.

Another valid path to good knowledge is insightful observation. A master practitioner observes a plant in its habitat. She watches how it grows and what types of animals can eat it. She may then test that observation personally, and eventually with appropriate patients. If the insight holds up, it might be taught. After a few hundred years, a disciple might include it in a book, at which point many other practitioners can test it and perhaps debate with it. Theories will arise pointing to other plants that show similar properties, and in testing, the theories themselves are tested and refined. While this doesn't constitute proof according to scientific methods, it carries the authenticity of two thousand years of keen intellectual attention and clinical application.

One more way good knowledge comes to us is through home cooking customs. This is the idea that A Million Grandmothers Can't Be Wrong. Scientists aren't allowed to say we might catch a common cold if we get wet in chilly weather unless studies prove it and a mechanism is demonstrated, but grandmothers have been insisting on it and adjusting neck scarves forever.

Akiko Iwasaki, PhD, is a professor of immunobiology focusing on viruses and our defenses against infection at the Yale School of Medicine. Her lab reported in 2015 that three markers for immune response are "greatly diminished" in response to the common cold rhinovirus as temperature falls even slightly within the nasal passageways.

This folk wisdom has now been proven, but that makes it no more true than it was before. In diet, this applies precisely—eat sauerkraut with fatty meats, have ginger when queasy, or snack on olives before dinner. There are deep wells of wisdom in the cultural traditions of world cuisines, practical wisdom that can be explained with the theories presented here.

These three paths to knowledge are dear to me—scientific study, insightful observation, and folk wisdom—none to the exclusion of the others. All three (and a few more) underlie what you can read here. They need to be integrated, for each is stronger by contributing to and receiving from each other. There is no need to be intimidated by any of it. The learning journey includes many details, but the main message remains:

Eat good food,

Learn what interests you,

Live life in good health.

THREE

Opening the Door to Food and Healing

Long ago, the masters of Chinese medicine taught that health is deeply individual. Each person must be considered with fresh interest, without preconceptions. This radically personal approach works well with our modern ideals of individualism. Keeping this in mind, the book you are holding offers a general tour of how diet and health work together, a discussion of what commonly goes awry, and recommendations of specific foods that can help the body remember good health. Pick and choose through the many ideas presented. The goal is to be in charge of yourself, to affirm your life through food choices and to be confident enough to embrace change in a clear and sensible way when needed.

As we begin the journey here, we need to introduce some terms and their meanings. Feel free to skip ahead if you are already familiar with them. If these terms are new to you, don't worry; their uses will become second nature to you as they are put to use and explained further.

Preliminaries

Every point of view has its particular preliminaries. When speaking of nutrition, for example, we think of *macronutrients*: proteins, carbohydrates, fats; and *micronutrients*: vitamins, minerals, enzymes, and so forth. Then there is awareness of stomach acids, glandular secretions, and the complex mechanics of digestion and assimilation. We all know about this to some degree, it's the common understanding of our culture, as reflected by government-mandated food labels. For example, we take it for granted that a banana can be good for someone who needs more potassium because bananas are high in that nutrient.

Another way of understanding food is offered in the dietary tradition of classical Chinese medicine. It's tremendously useful, whether eating to remain healthy or to recover good health. There is substantial overlap with the more mechanistic nutrition model of laboratory science. At first, the newer and older ways of understanding food may seem quite different, but as you live with them, the differences begin to soften. When we are able to integrate different ways of thinking, we are better equipped to implement wise choices. To become conversant in the ways that foods are assessed and classified in the dietary branch of classical Chinese medicine, we need to know a group of concepts. These are the preliminaries.

Building or Clearing

All foods help build our bodies, and many help clear toxins or wastes, but some foods are much more *building* while others are much more *clearing*. Foods high in protein, carbs or lipids (fats) are very *building*, while foods high in fiber or antioxidants are more *clearing*. This already begins an integration of the modern and classical points of view. We may discover that fruits and vegetables are high in antioxidants and fiber, but they've been known as *clearing* foods for two thousand years. Later in the book, you'll find more detail on which foods help in specific ways.

Warming or Cooling (Thermostatic Effect)

Everything we eat has multiple effects within us, one of which is the influence on our internal thermostat, beyond whether the food is *hot* or *cold* when we eat it. Most foods are classified as *warming* or *cooling*, but a few can be more extreme, classified as *hot* or *cold*. This means our internal functions warm or cool as we eat different foods, sometimes in ways we feel (sweating, for example) but more often going unnoticed. For dramatic examples, cayenne pepper is *hot* even if chilled, and celery is *cooling* even when served *hot*. Of course, cooking moderates the inherent characteristics (for example, celery is *cold* when raw, but only *cooling* when cooked).

Moistening or Drying

Hidden dehydration is very common, mostly ignored, and is a major factor beneath chronic illnesses and premature aging. Good hydration is far more than only drinking enough water; foods are just as important (including plenty of healthy oils). Some foods help the body with hydration. Examples of *moistening* foods include short grain rice, millet, corn, mushrooms, and some seafood. Other foods, including, for example, wheat, long grain rice, quinoa, diuretic drinks, and overuse of spices exert a *drying* effect. It may not seem very important, but effects of dietary habits become significant over time.

Directionality

Most people tend to think that if you eat a food, it's in there and gets evenly distributed, but that's not how foods work. Some exert an ascending effect, like garlic or asparagus, others seem to sink, like seeds and nuts.

There are *five directions* in food practice:

» Ascending

» Descending

» Centering

» Opening to the Exterior (spreading out)

» Astringing (holding or moving inward)

Taste

The taste of foods signals their energetic influence. As soon as we taste something, our bodies begin a cascade of responses, even if we don't swallow the food. For example, if we taste a wild berry and find it so bitter that we spit it out, our bodies are already responding internally. Even thinking of a strong taste can cause internal responses. Try thinking of biting a lemon, using all your imagination. You may find yourself salivating, or feel the pores on your skin pucker up. Taste itself influences internal functions.

Here, the word *taste* is a technical term—it includes the sense of taste but is also used in special ways. For example, sugar is sweet, of course, but so is rice, and even sometimes meat. What this means is that sweet foods are very building. Too much sugar can build too much body, rice has carbs that also help build. Meat, too, can be building. When herbalists and dietary specialists classify foods for taste, we are referring both to the common use of the word and at the same time using taste as a shorthand for how different foods function.

There are *six tastes* used in Chinese medicine dietetics:

» Sweet

» Sour

» Salty

» Pungent or Spicy

» Bitter

» Bland

Yes, bland is included as a taste, because the bland taste also performs a function (it helps clear dampness with a mild diuretic effect). More on all this later.

Yin and Yang

Yin and *yang* are abused terms, ready for revival by returning to their classical meanings. In food and health, *yin* refers to the physical aspects of the body, our physical substance. This includes our flesh and bones, blood and fluids (including the especially important fluids called *hormones*). *Yin* is cooling and moist; it is particularly important when we speak about the protective lining of the stomach and the small intestine.

Yang, on the other hand, is everything that is not material; *yang* is our warming and enlivening energy, our vital forces, including movement and circulation. We may have plenty of hormones, for example, but if they do not circulate properly, we will have problems. In this example, the hormones themselves are *yin* while their movement is *yang*. *Yin* and *yang* are inseparable but they not the same. All this will be discussed later with examples of how to work with it in our diets.

Qi

Qi (pronounced chee) is a term that cannot be easily translated, therefore it's best to borrow the word from Chinese. *Qi* refers to the potential to get something done or make a special connection. For example, if our digestive *qi* is weak we will have trouble digesting even very "healthy" foods. This is an important concept. Like so much in classical thinking, *qi* is a collective term that is often used in various specific ways. In dietary work we often speak of *lung qi*, ascending *pancreas-spleen qi*, or *kidney yang qi. Qi* overlaps with concepts of directionality and *yang*. It's about movement, communication and relationship, inside and out. To be simple, think of *qi* as the energy or the capacity to fulfill an internal health function. If *qi* is low or weak, functions will be slow or incomplete. Yes, it's a bit mysterious and intangible. If you prefer more mechanical explanations, just think of *qi* as a shorthand term for the collective functions of a specific organ or process.

The Three Levels of *Qi*

The early masters of Chinese medicine taught a system of correspondences based on Three Levels of *Qi*.

>> The middle is about nourishment, called the level of *Nutritive Qi* (*Ying Qi*). All food must be digested, so that is where I like to begin.

>> The deep level is the level of *Constitutional Qi* (*Yuan Qi*). Other translations of *yuan qi* are Source *Qi* or Ancestral *Qi*. This includes our genetic inheritance, reproductive health (the ability to pass on our genetics, whether we do or not), bone and marrow status, and other very deep aspects of health. In a word, our constitutional health.

>> The upper or surface level is called the level of *Protective Qi* (*Wei Qi*). This includes our immune capability and other factors of staying safe, including the ability to sweat, to face threats, and so forth.

With a little practice, this way of seeing things can be used at home for great benefit.

Organ Connections

The Three Levels of *Qi* is an early historical model. In classical thought, new ideas are layered on top of earlier ones rather than replacing them (in stark contrast to modern thinking, which expects to replace older thought with what is new). Categorizing foods as supporting one or more of the Three Levels of *Qi* began more than two thousand years ago. About one thousand years later, the focus shifted to the internal organs that reside in or govern the levels of *qi*. They are given the familiar names (liver, kidneys, stomach, etc.), but are seen as collective concepts that include the anatomical organ and the physical, emotional, and spiritual connections those organs make.

Foods are said to have special affinity with certain organs. For example, almonds have a lung and large intestine affinity, while cabbage has affinity with stomach and pancreas-spleen. *Affinity* is a beautiful word, but for clarity's sake I use the word *connection*. The affinity-connection properties of foods can get complicated. Cabbage, for example, is classified only with stomach and pancreas-spleen affinities, but it also strongly affects the liver and gallbladder functions. In this book I mention affinity-connections when they are particularly important and useful.

The Five Elemental Phases

Another historical lens that remains very useful is often called the Five Element system, but the original term, *wu xing*, really means *five movements*. Some practitioners call them phases. Rather than elements in the sense of the Periodic Table (nearly immutable), the Five Elemental Phases describe characteristic patterns in the way things shift and interact, including food and health. Each phase includes personality characteristics and internal organ associations. The Five Elemental Phases are:

» Earth

» Metal

» Water

» Wood

» Fire

Foods have been classified according to the Elemental Phases, but don't worry, references are explained in context as needed.

The Law of Signature

The law of signature Is the Oldest method of food associations still in use, connecting us with humanity's earliest experiences in the natural world. Living in nature, early people must have looked at plants and thought, "That plant is tough, hanging on to a rocky cliff like that. I'd love to be that tough, I wonder if I can gather some of its nature if I *eat* it?" (Capers are an example of a food plant that can grow on cliff edges, seeming to live on almost nothing.) Later, "I have chilly aches in my neck and limbs. I'll eat a warming plant that has lots of branches, like arms and legs." (Cinnamon twigs are like that.) And, "I've been told I'm a bit blood deficient or borderline anemic, maybe red beets will help me build blood." (Beets indeed contain a variety of nutrients that specifically help build blood.)

The law of signature is ancient and instinctual, nearly lost by the deification of rational thought. To an open mind, modern rational thinking layers on top of the mythic and poetic without conflict. The law of signature can be an opening to a more intuitive relationship with foods, alongside the many newer methods we use to understand our lives as consciously eating beings.

The Influence of Climate

Chinese medicine rests on a deep appreciation of nature. The language is poetic, and the influence of climate is considered both literal and metaphoric. Formal teaching includes Six Climatic Factors that cause health problems: *cold, heat, summer heat, dampness, dryness* and *wind.* For our purposes, summer heat and dryness are included in the discussion of good hydration (see chapter six). We can then more simply focus on the other four.

Internal Cold

Everyone feels cold sometimes; that's normal when the weather is chilly, or if you forgot to carry an extra layer of clothing. Our bodies protect us, and we can usually find ways to warm up without problems. But if cold penetrates within, it can take up residence. This type of cold is called *internal cold.* The way the body then responds depends on an individual's constitutional strength, current health, emotional status, and of course, diet.

Because food and drink go right into the center of our torso, they have a particularly strong influence on internal temperature regulation. The stomach doesn't work well below body temperature; digestion waits until cool foods have been sufficiently warmed. Cold slows things down. In fact, *cold* is also used to describe any bodily function that is slower than it should be, even if not caused by physical cold.

If not well prepared, physical cold can leave us more vulnerable to the common cold. Current science confirms that the rhinoviruses believed to cause the common cold are far more successful if our nasal passageways drop even a few degrees below our core body temperature, and that raising our breathing passageway temperature back those few degrees strongly enhances immunity. Based on classical Chinese medicine, similar studies looking into the introduction of cold to the digestion would also yield important results. Internal cold can spread from the digestive tract, causing serious problems in many parts of our system.

Symptoms and conditions of long-residing internal cold include stomach pain, fatigue, watery diarrhea, dull achy joints, cold hands and feet, runny nose or postnasal drip.

Cold can be introduced by cold foods (iced water, ice cream, iced coffee), or raw foods (sushi, salads, sprouts, too much fruit in the wrong season or climate). To resolve internal cold, have cooked food, drink plain hot water, use warming kitchen spices (ginger, cinnamon, clove, star anise, turmeric, cumin, oregano, rosemary, scallions, sometimes garlic, if severe), eat stews and soups including chicken broth and beef bone broth.

The overall strategy for addressing internal cold is to eliminate exposure to more cold while eating warming foods aimed at the affected locations by using your understanding of the directionality of different foods.

Damaging Heat

Life relies upon warmth, but if internal heat becomes excessive, serious damage to health can occur. Heat damage can include all types of inflammation and consequent tissue damage, blood pressure problems, sleep disturbances, emotional issues, irritation or anger, and more.

The balance of cold and heat is not simple; often, excess heat arises as a natural body response to internal cold, requiring skilled detective work to discern which is the original problem (and thus which needs to be resolved at the deepest level to not only relieve symptoms but resolve the problem fully).

It's possible to resolve excess heat (often called *fire*) by avoiding foods that irritate or heat too much (hot spices, alcohol, coffee, nightshades, chocolate, garlic, onions), eat more *yin* supportive foods (grains, porridges, fish, seafood, warmed sprouts, cooked green vegetables, nuts and seeds) and correct the directional problems that are present (use legumes and root vegetables).

Lifestyle is also extremely important, beyond the limits of diet itself. Sleep is a *yin* (cooling) factor; sleep that is insufficient or shifted to very late night and into the morning contributes to heat conditions (or sabotages their resolution). Stress and emotions are also crucial; irritation, anger, and "hot-headedness" can result from heat in the physical body, or "hot" emotions can contribute to that heat, especially when it influences cravings for unhelpful food and drink. Lifestyle adjustments must be included with diet and any medical intervention to achieve full and lasting success.

Dampness

Dampness refers to any condition where internal fluids build up without being cleared and refreshed. Dampness can be water weight around the middle or thighs, edema in the ankles or face; it can collect in the joints, block the sense organs, and it is part of any swelling. Dampness can be apparent or hidden. It is an internal housekeeping issue. Dampness gradually and steadily rises if our bodies fall behind in clearing and cleaning, if we continue to eat the wrong things or feel chronically stressed and lose sleep. Dampness slows us down, clouds our mental clarity, sets the stage for accumulations and growths, and leaves us more vulnerable to getting ill. As our bodies ramp up to try to handle the accumulations (often with heat), dampness can be a causative factor for many common imbalances and chronic illnesses.

Related to dampness is *phlegm*. Phlegm can arise in response to a common cold or as a progression of long-term dampness. Phlegm can also be apparent or hidden.

Along with overeating, eating too late at night, eating when stressed or when standing or walking, there are three key food groups that easily contribute to dampness if overused: sugar, dairy, and gluten. Dampness very often accumulates as a kind of insulation against inflammation caused by hot irritants; this means that hot spices, alcohol, and so forth also can cause dampness.

Foods that help clear dampness include ginger, scallion, (warmed) sprouts, barley, non-glutinous grains, snow peas or snap peas, fermented foods, mushrooms, and the warming (not hot) spices. A good strategy is always needed. For dampness, it's essential to avoid damp-causing foods (sugar, dairy, gluten, and dietary irritants) while adding some of the foods that help clear dampness. Because treating dampness clears old fluids, we need to provide fresh fluids. Soups are very important.

The Disruptions Called Wind

Wind is a classical term describing any type of sudden disruption of health. Sometimes this disruption lingers, taking up residence, so to speak. Wind is used to talk about colds or flu, pain, stiffness, dizziness, even seizures and strokes.

Before applying specific food strategies to clear *wind* it is most important to strengthen basic health. The disruptions called wind can enter and take hold if we are somehow weakened or particularly inflexible. We must stay flexible and willing to change with circumstances such as the shifting weather, ups and downs in personal fortunes, and even external political events. From a dietary view, staying flexible in body and mind relies upon being good at producing enough healthy blood, which in turn comes from eating healthy foods and digesting them well. The entire system is involved in this, from our kidneys at the base of our health, to our stomach and intestines, to the organs of metabolism that include the pancreas and spleen, as well as the liver (which stores blood) and its partner the gallbladder (which holds the liver's digestive secretions) and the heart and lungs, which complete the role of blood enrichment and proper circulation. When all is working well, based on personally wise food choices, the disruptions called wind can be managed with relative ease.

These are the preliminaries we need in order to truly understand food for our eating pleasure and good health. This is the journey of *Welcoming Food*.

FOUR

The General Guidelines

Improving health and happiness is a unique path for each of us, and it is wise to be wary of any advice that claims to apply to everyone. General guidelines can be useful for general eating, however, and provide us with a starting place. Here are some fundamental concepts that can be applied when cooking for yourself or family members.

The Goal of Healthy Eating Is Overall Good Health

Many begin to think about diet with a specific focus such as losing weight, clearing pain, or feeling more energetic, only to discover that good results can be fleeting. In fact, some dietary plans, trying too hard to achieve one isolated thing, can actually damage underlying health. Remember, food is like medicine; unwanted side effects are possible.

Developing healthier food habits that you enjoy is the best way to avoid the yo-yo dieting problem—new hopes alternating with old habits. In creating your plan for good health, you'll discover that improving digestion is the best place to begin.

Listen to these comments from clients:

> "When I focus on better digestion, my body naturally loses that extra weight."

> "When I learned how to eat for better digestion, my reflux pain went away on its own, and when I occasionally stray, a small amount of medicine does the trick. Before, I took a ton of medicine and the pain was still there almost every day!"

Good digestion is the secret to good overall health. As you embrace this principle, you will see lasting results.

Eat Real Foods That Your Body Can Recognize and Digest Well

Different foods digest in different ways. The key to good health is to eat meals that your personal digestion can handle well. Digestive capacity varies by individual, and changes over time. Our bodies know how to digest even complicated meals, if the foods are real and our digestion is strong. But if we are sick or have very delicate digestion, often even a tiny amount of the wrong food can cause a loss of appetite, pain, distention, or other symptoms. In these cases, it is essential to learn what we can eat without triggering problems, even if it means our diet is very restricted. That is the place to start. Sometimes, early in our healing process, a precise game has to be played to get enough nourishment from small amounts of simple food. When we are finally eating without bad reactions, our bellies can begin to heal. Soon, a fuller diet will become possible. The key is to eat real, unadulterated foods that your digestion can recognize and knows how to digest instinctively, whether for general health maintenance or for actively healing specific problems.

Add Helpful Foods and Avoid Foods That Are Hurting You

If we continue to eat what has been hurting us, just adding recommended foods will not be enough. Every dietary adjustment should include both "what to add" and "what to avoid."

Two Quick Stories

A patient arrived and showed me her picture from two years before. She was now much thinner and visibly happier than in the photo. She said that she still didn't know enough about how to eat, but she had lost all that weight simply by stopping her habit of eating ice cream every night after dinner.

Another had nearly the same story, but for him it was two things: "I used to have pasta every day, now I have none, and I used to eat late, now I eat absolutely nothing after 8 p.m., ever."

In both cases abstaining from what was causing or sustaining their weight problem was enough to lose the excess. They were smart, they stopped doing what was hurting them. They came for dietary sessions to learn how to improve more deeply.

For many people, this process is more difficult and more tools are needed, but the principle can be helpful for everyone: avoiding our personal problem foods is as important as adding helpful ones.

Often it is enough to simply stop eating what causes (or sustains) our problems.

Do Not Be Seduced by Superfoods

We live in a vast industrial marketplace fueled by advanced advertising that promises instant gratification. The food industry would like to process and package all our foods (cheaper ingredients, higher profit margins), and then sell us packaged superfoods to fix what goes wrong. The health food (and supplement) industry often employs the same tactics.

In the clinic, it's common to hear: "I want to be healthier, but please don't ask me to change much. Is there something I can take, or eat, without giving anything up?" This is the modern medical fantasy. Turn this thinking around to find your power. "What can I do for myself so that I don't need to take as much medicine, or so the medicines I do take work better?"

The key is becoming aware of our true state of health and learning how to eat to address our individual concerns. Simply adding "superfoods" does not help us if we continue the food habits that got us into trouble in the first place. My advice? Avoid superfood fads, and abstain from food habits that are bad for you while making good meals with beneficial foods prepared in delicious ways.

Listen to All the Grandmothers

There's a lot of wisdom in traditional cuisines. I call it "grandmother wisdom". We can do pretty well following grandmotherly advice: *eat well, stay warm, get enough rest*. Picture a family restaurant in Italy, France, Mexico, China, Japan, India, or any place with a strong traditional cuisine (great meals in wonderful tiny eateries all over the world have deeply influenced my views of food). The grandmother is cooking in the back, and she has strong ideas about the food she makes. If you order one dish, two dishes may arrive ("This *always* goes with that!"). If you order things that don't work together, the offending combination just never arrives. Diet is part of a lifestyle.

Include Building and Clearing Foods in Your Diet

There are times when traditional cuisine or grandmother wisdom isn't enough. A more specific healing strategy is needed to fix a bump in the road. One of the dietary mistakes most commonly made (and a serious one, too) is mistaking when to *build* and when to *clear*.

Balancing building and clearing is central to the art of diet. Proteins, carbohydrates and fats (along with vitamins and minerals) are needed for the body to build muscles, bones, blood, fluids and hormones. Building foods provide an energetic message to *hold* and *solidify*. These nutrients are basic and necessary, but if building foods are overused, stagnation can develop. From there, we may encounter a host of unwanted conditions: excess weight, inflammation, hormonal imbalances, cardiovascular problems, joint problems, and so forth.

Clearing foods offer the natural balance to building foods. Foods that include fiber help clearing (whole grains, legumes, green vegetables, spices, fruits, nuts, seeds, and tubers like sweet potatoes). Bitter foods provide an energetic message to *let go* and *clear* (broccoli rabe, dandelion leaf, endive, radicchio, chicory lettuce, bitter melon, and more). Two cases from the clinic will help explain how important this can be.

A client arrived, a busy career woman wanting to have a baby. Fertility was elusive despite an "all good" from her doctor. She reported having "an excellent diet," but it was the wrong kind of excellent: vegetable juices for breakfast and salads for lunch. She was slender and seemed vibrant, but her pulses were weak and slow. Her diet and hopes were at odds. Juices and salads make a clearing, cooling diet while pregnancy requires building and internal warmth. After changing to a richer diet of cooked foods, she conceived after four months and is now a mother.

Another person, presenting with chronic Lyme disease, had gone through multiple courses of antibiotic treatment without success. Sleep was disturbed, emotions were taut, appetite was weak, energy was very low. Following one cleansing diet after another, he was feeling weaker and weaker. He needed to build strength with real foods, skillfully cooked with spices to aid weakened digestion. After about nine months of careful building, he was strong enough to make treatment of the original infection possible.

Apply Focused Intention When Selecting, Cooking, and Eating Food

Intention is a precise communication of mind, heart, and body (action). It combines inspiration, knowledge, and discipline. Intention needs exercise to become strong, and effective intention is never vague. When you understand more about the basic principles and qualities of food, you can develop clear intention when selecting what to eat. "This is to build me up—my strength, energy, bones, juices, muscle mass, self-esteem." Or, "This is to help me clear stuff I've been slowly gathering for years—some extra weight but also accumulations and toxins gathering with-in me that may cause problems now, or later."

When exercised consistently, strong intention leads to intuition, and our efforts become spontaneous.

Very clear intention is so powerful it can sometimes neutralize damaging food. There is a legendary story of a master who accepts an invitation to bring his class to the home of the grandmother of one of his students. "Thank you so much for teaching my granddaughter—she loves what you teach and all her new friends. Here, have a sugar cookie. They've just come out of the oven!" The students froze, all eyes on the teacher. But he didn't hesitate. "Thank you, I'd love one. They smell delicious. The smell of your kitchen reminds me of my own grandmother's cooking, a feeling I'd thought I'd never meet again." He reaches for a cookie, pauses unnoticeably to whisper, "This too will nourish me," before he eats it and beams at the cook. The secret is clear intention, and…just have one. Problems will arise if indulgences become habit. Intention is not a fantasy; intention is a principle that guides action.

Apply Focused Intention to All the Dietary Knowledge You Are Developing

Until we spontaneously (and correctly) know what to eat and how to prepare it, we can practice by applying clear intention to the dietary knowledge we are developing. Each of the preliminaries introduced in the previous section can be the focus of intention as you shop, cook, and enjoy food:

> » Building or Clearing
>
> » Warming or Cooling (Thermostatic Effect)
>
> » Moistening or Drying
>
> » Directionality
>
> » Effect Based on Taste
>
> » *Yin* and *Yang*
>
> » Three Levels of *Qi*
>
> » Organ Connection

» The Five Elements (Phases)

» The Law of Signature

Commonly, we select food with only two things in mind: what we like and what we think has nutrients we need, but each of the above categories can be the focus of your intention. It's not as complicated as it may seem. As you read through Book 1 and make recipes from Book 2, you will learn how to select foods based on your growing knowledge of their energetics and your increasing awareness of what works for *you*.

Using Building and Clearing as an Example to Understand Focusing Intention

To understand this more concretely, let's look at *building* and *clearing* with specific foods.

» Tubers such as sweet potatoes have a sweet taste (building), are rich in carbohydrates (building), and include excellent fiber (clearing, moving).

» Legumes, seeds, and nuts are all high in protein, carbs, and oils (building) and have plenty of fiber (clearing) and a descending energy (moving, clearing). Their oils are building but also aid peristalsis (moving). Many natural foods are well balanced.

» Whole grains contain good fiber (clearing) to balance their carbs, oils, and protein (building). In contrast, refined grains such as white rice or white flour contain very little fiber; they are far more building than clearing.

» Meats, dairy and eggs are high in protein (building) and oils (building) but contain no fiber. Distinctly clearing foods should be eaten alongside these foods or in the next meal.

Imagine a breakfast of eggs, hash-brown potatoes, white bread toast, orange juice and coffee with milk and sugar. There are plenty of protein, oils and carbs, but nothing that is descending or clearing. Coffee is a laxative, true, but much less so with sugar (building, and binding in the intestines) and milk (building, and difficult to digest in a meal that includes orange juice). Such a breakfast will certainly satisfy hunger through the whole morning, but because it is slow to digest and lacks clearing foods, this kind of eating can easily lead to stagnation, poor digestion, weight gain and tiredness. The same problem occurs with a meat and potatoes dinner; the meat is very building and the potatoes provide carbs with a "hold to the center" energy. Because the meal is heavy to digest, often a sweet dessert is desired to provide a boost. Sweets slow digestion even more when combined with a hearty meal, easily leading to stagnation if repeated regularly.

Adding Directionality Helps Fine-Tune Building and Clearing

Vegetables, fruits, and spices are highly directional. They bring *moving* energy to meals and contain various types of fiber that aid clearing. Some vegetables and spices provide *ascending* moving energy (asparagus, celery, rosemary, cinnamon), some *spreading out* moving energy (collard, kale, chard, oregano, and again cinnamon), some *consolidating inward* energy (cabbage, broccoli, brussels sprouts, salt, lemon), and some descending-cooling-clearing energy (bitter greens such as broccoli rabe, chicory, radicchio, endive, dandelion greens, bitter melon, thyme). Looking at this from another point of view, the antioxidants in vegetables and fruits clear toxins at the cellular (chemical) level.

Cooked or Raw: The Traditional Bias Against Raw Foods

Until modern plumbing brought reliably treated water into the home, there was no safe way to wash vegetables for raw consumption. Farms used manure as fertilizer, and human waste management was not sufficient to safeguard drinking or farm water. Unboiled water and raw foods were potentially deadly. It's not surprising, then, that many traditional cultures developed deep taboos around raw or undercooked foods.

In the late 19th century, scientists discovered that cholera and typhoid were spread by contaminated water. This led to the development of modern water treatment. At roughly the same time, micronutrients were being discovered in food. Together, clean water and enough food variety to supply sufficient vitamins and minerals revolutionized public health, virtually eliminating deficiency diseases and some of the worst infectious diseases (in societies willing and able to provide these basic services). Once clean water was readily available, raw foods could be safely incorporated into our diets, but more subtle questions about the health effects of cooked or raw foods remain.

Cooking Makes Digestion Much Easier, Supporting All Aspects of Health

Proponents of raw food diets correctly point out that vegetables and fruits have more nutrients when raw than when cooked (with some exceptions). But it is also true that cooked foods are much easier to digest and assimilate. Ease of digestion is key. When digestion is challenged or stressed, fewer nutrients can be assimilated. Our focus should be on how foods interact with our bodies, not on their abstract nutrition as measured in laboratories. To put the two views together, a few more points are needed.

Raw food can be strongly clearing, but sometimes too much so, leaving us feeling cold and depleted. Salads, for example, can help weight loss because they contain few building foods while the fiber and cold temperature exert a descending and clearing energy. What isn't seen easily in lab testing is that raw foods (including salads) can easily introduce too much cold to the digestive tract, slowing digestive functions, eventually leading to serious problems for many people. (For some, cold food can *cause* weight gain—rather than the weight loss expected with clearing foods—because foods with cold energetics slow digestion.) In short, no part of digestion is improved by the introduction of cold. For best digestion, cook most of your food.

Cooking Aids Digestion, but Overcooking Isn't Good, Either

Cooking foods strongly aids digestion, but overcooking drains foods of both their nutrients and their natural message. Imagine asparagus cooked just until it turns bright green and is barely tender, then picture overcooked asparagus—mushy, dull, dispirited. Raw asparagus is taxing to digest, but overcooked asparagus lacks nutrients and energy. Perfectly cooked asparagus offers its nourishment and its uplifting, invigorating fresh energy full of complex flavors. How you cook it (steaming, sautéing, baking, etc.) aims a food's natural energetics more precisely (more on cooking methods in Book 2, *Recipes and Kitchen Practice*). Cook your food skillfully to fine-tune its benefits and, of course, maximize your eating pleasure.

Individual Needs Must Always Be Considered

When we are very young, very old, or when digestion is weak for any reason, it is important to make foods easier to digest by cooking them longer. A major stressor for many children today is that they are fed solid foods too soon, stimulating their delicate digestions to mature too quickly. Babies and young children naturally have relatively weak digestive systems. Their food should be gentle and appropriate. Commercial baby food is not necessary—parents of young children can take some of what they're cooking before adding spices, cook it a bit longer on its own, or mash it for toddlers.

Simple, long-cooked food is also important for anyone who is sick, whether just for a day or in a long illness. Convalescing food should be gentle and easy to digest, similar in principle to appropriate food for the young.

Digestive fire naturally declines as we age. The exact age when this happens is not the same for everyone, just as menopause or any other milestone of aging is an individual experience within fairly broad age brackets. At some point, however, our bodies change significantly, and our diet should change, too. We want our diets to support us through all stages of our lives.

A common mistake the elderly make in modern culture is ignoring this traditional advice, attempting to live "beyond their digestion" as a token of staying young and vital. Someone may boast, "I'm still eating like when I was forty," but healthy eating should change as we change.

For those who love good food, this does not need to be bad news; long cooked foods are not "adult baby food". At least once a day include a meal that is appropriate for long cooking, for example, have vegetable soup rather than salad, beef stew rather than medium-rare steak, or congee rather than steamed rice (two congee recipes are included Book 2).

Examine (Honestly) Your Own Diet from Multiple Points of View

One of the most powerful things we can do for ourselves is to understand the characteristics of our regular diet. Is your regular diet roughly balanced in building/clearing, warming/cooling, directionality, effects of our favored tastes, *yin* and *yang*? Does your diet work with the three levels of *qi*? How do your favorite foods connect with your various internal organs?   Two examples from recent patients will help make this consideration more concrete:

"I like meat and potatoes, but I didn't realize how much more building than clearing they are. I like a green salad, but I guess the blue cheese dressing pretty much negates the benefit of the lettuce for clearing purposes." This person wanted to lose a few pounds, and to clear up internal housekeeping issues including achy joints, gout, and periodic kidney stones. He would benefit from more whole grains, cooked green vegetables, smaller portions of meat, and snacks of fresh fruit and nuts, similar to what is often called a Mediterranean diet.

"I'm a vegan, I think that's the best diet in every way, but people say I'm too skinny. I see that my diet is far more clearing than building, especially because I like to eat a lot of raw food. I do eat beans, but I can't seem to gain weight or stay warm in the winter." This person may benefit from white rice in place of brown (brown rice is too clearing for her), cooking all her food and including warming kitchen herbs and spices.

When shopping, cooking and eating, have clear intention about the balance of building and clearing. Meals should not be completely even; tip the balance slightly in favor one or the other based on individual needs and according to the seasons.

A meal that is more building than clearing helps us build strength but must have some clearing aspect to avoid stagnation either in digestion or in the blood (stagnation is sluggishness in function and can include arterial plaque buildups). This type of meal favors protein while including healthy carbs and green vegetables. Here are a few examples of meals that favor building but include some clearing qualities:

» Chicken, white rice, string beans, with olive oil, sea salt and kitchen herbs

» Beef, lamb or pork, sweet potato, kale dressed with olive oil and sea salt

» Pasta, lentils, broccoli rabe, with olive oil, lemon juice, salt, fresh basil and bit of fresh black pepper

Fine-tune these examples based on individual needs. White rice could be combined with wild rice (white rice is building; wild rice is clearing). Animal foods are chosen not only for preference but for their own characteristics. Pasta (wheat) may be replaced with rice noodle or another substitute to be less inflammatory, if needed.

A meal that is more clearing than building helps us lose weight or clear internal congestions, but it must protect our strength in the process. This type of meal favors whole grains, root vegetables, legumes and greens but can include some animal foods if desired. Here are a few examples of meals that favor clearing but still include supportive building qualities:

> » Chickpea curry with peas, zucchini and kale over brown rice
>
> » White fish with celery, mung bean sprouts and chard over steamed millet
>
> » Tofu with mushrooms and broccoli with combined grain of buckwheat kernels and long grain white rice

Learn to Think in Strategies

Good eating begins with meal planning, whether done in advance, at the market, or just while gazing into the refrigerator. Looking at a menu in a restaurant is also meal planning. In whatever way you do your planning, it's good to consider how every meal will fit into your overall strategy to improve or sustain health.

Focus first on making meals that are well balanced (for example, don't have bread as appetizer and then have rice with the meal). A basic meal includes "a grain, a green, and a protein". Later, learn to aim meals for your personal needs (which grain, which green vegetable, which protein). With a clear strategy, even occasional meals that aren't perfect for you won't cause more than a temporary setback.

Treat the Person, Not the Condition

When dietary clients arrive in the clinic, they very often identify with their Western medical diagnosis. "I have high blood pressure." "I am diabetic." "I have depression." "I have Lyme disease, and it'll never go away!" Then I hear, "What is the diet for blood pressure?" Or for diabetes, depression, or Lyme syndrome. Living in the modern world, it's a lesson we must learn over and over: the best approach is not a treatment for a "condition" but a full assessment of the individual and the unique strategy that person can employ to recover their natural health. The oral tradition of classical Chinese medicine includes the beautiful axiom: *Treat the person, not the condition.*

As complexities increase, our health is handed over to experts and specialists, too often leaving us feeling disempowered and doubtful if our kitchen knowledge can make any difference for our health and well-being.

The details of our bodies' functions are endless; we are too complex for our own minds to know. Luckily, we don't need to know everything. The living body knows what to do. Problems arise, sustained by lifestyle and emotional habits, but with some help our bodies are amazingly ready to return to health if skillfully nudged in the right direction. With this in mind, we need a simplified way to understand what to do, trusting that the infinite wisdom of the body will do the rest.

Understanding Ourselves?

There is a wonderful teaching about the neurology of worms. The common worm has 302 neurons (brain cells), connected by perhaps 7,000 synapses. That's a lot, but it's not an unimaginable amount. It is conceivable that all 302 neurons could be known and even all 7,000 connections understood, but the intelligence experienced by 302 neurons will never be powerful enough to understand those 302 neurons. Some hypothetically intelligent being (or human scientist) may come to comprehensively understand those neurons and connections, but clearly worms don't have the mental horsepower to understand worms.

Humans are very intelligent, with wonderful powers of understanding, but our brains have 100 billion neurons, our bodies have 37 trillion cells (plus a trillion resident microbes). Our scientific knowledge should be held in perspective. We can know ourselves as a king knows his kingdom: we may be in charge, but most of what is going on always remains beyond our awareness.

Tune the Three Centers of Health

Traditionally, in order to simplify our work with the web of health connections, the inner body is grouped into three centers. These are known in Chinese medicine as the three centers or *burners* of the torso:

> » The middle center is the area below the ribs but above the navel.

> » The upper center is the area above the breathing diaphragm (the bottom of the ribcage).

» The lower center is the area below the navel.

Learning to connect with and tune the three centers is the basis of holistic medicine using diet and herbs. Mastery is a long study, but the fundaments are powerful, and can be learned and implemented easily. Here is the framework:

» The middle center digests food. I like to start with the middle because this is where food goes first: the stomach and upper intestine, the pancreas-spleen (considered together), liver and gallbladder. Taking good care of the middle improves overall health because all nourishment depends on good digestion.

» The lower center is about elimination and reproductive health. In Chinese medicine, this includes the kidneys, bladder and lower intestines. Being able to clear out the bowels and bladder is essential to health; if weak here, no healthy cleansing anywhere in the body can be successful. The lower center also includes hormone secreting glands that are essential to the body's deepest health. The status of the lower center controls the health of the body's foundation (genetics, bones, bone marrow, reproductive system, brain) and longevity. Think of the lower center as the lower belly, occupying the entire pelvis, like a big basin.

» The upper center is about good breathing and immunity. The chest invites air in, mixes breath into our blood, then sends this enlivened blood to every cell in our body. The upper center is the center of respiration and circulation. It is also the first defense against airborne germs because the outside world enters the body through the nose, throat, eyes, ears, and mouth. The upper center comprises the chest, throat, and head.

Foods that connect with the different centers (and the ways to use them) will be described as the book progresses.

The Law of Signature Is the Oldest Guiding Method Still in Use

As mentioned in the Preliminaries, the oldest guiding system of food correspondences is known as the *law of signature*. It's a fundamental idea from the beginning of history that can still be applied intelligently today.

We have become so accustomed to thinking of foods as only collections of nutrients that some people have stopped eating foods altogether, surviving on carefully crafted nutrient mixes, as if life on Earth is no different than life in a space capsule. Perhaps this kind of eating is a logical extension of nutrient science, but I hope proponents will open their minds to the full functions of food (such as directionality, cooling/warming, social bonding, human pleasure, and so forth), and decide to return to Earth.

Foods are more than their nutrients; they have characteristics. Since ancient times, people have looked at plants, noticing that some need cold weather, some need warmth. Some can gather moisture in a desert, others thrive in swamps. Some grow very gradually, while others shoot up overnight. Each is different. Built into our bones is the instinct that we can absorb some of a plant's vitality by eating it, or, if you prefer more modern language, everything we eat influences us to some extent. This idea that every food has a signature energy of its own has been tested and refined in the Chinese medicine tradition for thousands of years. It is an important aspect of dietary practice that is especially helpful for returning a sense of nature to our kitchen and dinner plates. Science explains; mythic thinking sparks understanding. Both are essential ingredients of a good meal.

When will each point of view be most fruitful? With time a knack develops, a know-how about when to think in terms of building/clearing, three centers of *qi*, warming/cooling, moistening/drying, directionality, five element theory, nutrition science, and so forth. It's common to see motivated people become overly focused on one point of view. The required flexibility grows with interest and experience.

Beginners and Masters Like to Keep Things Simple

If dietary advice ever seems confusing, remember these simple guidelines:

» Eat real foods that digest well for you.

   No matter how good a food is supposed to be for you, if it's not digesting well, or you really hate the taste, it's not for you at the present time. Specific ways to aid digestion, or what to eat instead, are covered in later chapters.

» Get rest, avoid cold, and maintain a skillfully open heart.

   When well rested and happy, everything works better, including digestion. Don't abuse this gift, however, food choices also do matter.

» Enjoy the foods that your body also enjoys.

   The highest skill of a cook is to make healthy eating delicious and satisfying.

That's all that's needed. But because life can be complicated, there may be reasons to add more precision to your plan. As you do, remember these points:

» Have focused intention. Shop, cook and eat according to what you are trying to do: build more or clear more, harmonize directionality, regulate warming or cooling, hydrate better, nourish the three centers, support the *qi* of specific organs, and so forth.

» Be wary of extreme diets. Nourish all the various aspects of overall health. As we learn how different foods work with different parts of our internal health, it's easier to understand why we need variety in our diets.

» If in doubt, it is always helpful to focus on good digestion. Healthy digestion is the centerpiece of all health.

Now that we have an overview, let's look in more detail at our foods and good digestion. The journey begins with appetite.

FIVE

Whetting the Appetite

A true appetizer helps our digestion welcome food. In Chinese medicine, this is called *opening the stomach*. Appetizers are not just small portions of something yummy to snack on while waiting for or preparing food. A true appetizer fulfills four digestive functions:

» Stimulate salivation, signaling the digestive organs to prepare for food

» Clear food stagnation, if present (previous food moving too slowly through the digestion process)

» Help food descend (reflux, for example, is a problem of stomach energy rising rather than descending, see box on page 48-49).

» Gently raise *stomach fire* to prepare us to digest proteins and provide that pleasant hungry feeling (stimulating just the right amount of stomach acid)

There is enormous accumulated wisdom in traditional cuisines. Often traditional appetizers work well as true appetizers, but sometimes not, and the difference is important. Consult this guide to appetizers that fulfill the role of opening the stomach to welcome food.

Type of Appetizer	Examples and Explanations
Bitter Nibbles	Olives, Artichokes
Brined and Pickled Things Brining is the process of transforming and preserving foods in a salt water soak.	Olives are brined (as well as being originally bitter). Artichokes are sometimes brined (and are also bitter in taste).
Pickling uses salt and vinegar with herbs & spices.	Pickled beets, carrots, green tomatoes, cucumber pickles. Dill (often used for pickling) promotes digestive secretions including bile.

Root Vegetables and Crunchy Things	Root vegetables (like carrots, radishes, daikon or jicama) aid descending energy, essential for good stomach function. If digestion is weak all food should be cooked, but for those with plenty of digestive strength, raw (or barely cooked) carrots are a wonderful appetizer. They are descending and remarkably good at clearing food stagnation. Further, the crunchiness strongly stimulates stomach function through vibration at the jaw (key acupoints for the stomach meridian are located on the jaw). Crunchiness is a very important aspect to include, if digestive strength allows it. Carrots are crunchy and sweet, aiding stomach and pancreas, while the sharp taste of radishes is excellent for helping stagnation from fats (particularly helpful for those who eat a lot of cheese).
Fermented Things	Small amounts of naturally fermented foods wake the liver and gallbladder, preparing secretions that promote healthy appetite, move food stagnation, help descend stomach energetics and prepare for digestion of the meal to come.

There are fermented foods from all over the world. Some people like food adventures, others prefer staying closer to home. Select accordingly.

Fermented appetizers include: sauerkraut, miso soup or other miso things, kefir, pickles (mentioned above), kombucha, and small amounts of wine or rice wine. |
| A Note on Wine | Alcohol is a problem for many people and cannot be recommended without a warning. Those who can't safely drink wine should certainly avoid it. For those who can, it is useful specifically as an appetizer in very small amounts before a meal. Visualize the traditional sherry glass used for an aperitif, 1 to 1.5 ounces. In Asia, the favored aperitif to aid digestion is plum wine; in the West it is traditionally sherry. Both are fairly sweet; in small amounts they stimulate appetite, and prepare pancreas and spleen secretions while harmonizing those organs with liver and gallbladder. In large amounts, however, they tax the same systems and cause disharmony between liver and pancreas-spleen. Since alcohol does increase appetite, it should be noted that it can lead to weight gain (or sabotage a weight-loss plan), not because of its calories but through the way it stimulates the sensation of hunger.

Cooking with wine (or rice wine, etc.) can bring its benefits with virtually no alcohol for many who abstain from drinking, as well as for children. |

Stimulating salivation is a very important part of opening the stomach. Saliva is produced after the clear fluid is sorted from food and drink in the stomach and absorbed into the system. This clear fluid then needs to ascend to the mouth area, transported by good metabolism. Stimulating salivation with appetizers completes this cycle (as the saliva enters the food and returns down to the stomach). It is important that our diets avoid overheating or drying the stomach with too many spicy or dehydrating foods.

Foods that stimulate saliva include:

» Bitter tasting greens (endive, radicchio, escarole, parsley, etc.)

» Carrots, celery and other crunchy, chewy foods. As mentioned in the chart above, crunchy foods stimulate the stomach and saliva, beginning the process of digestion and assimilation. If nothing is chewy or crunchy in your "good" diet, you will likely crave chips or something less good late in the day for evening bingeing.

» Apples, pears and Asian pears

» Citrus, in moderate or small amounts

» All spices move fluids; best for stimulating saliva are fresh ginger, fennel seed, star anise, cardamom pod, or caraway seed. Spices can be used in dishes, infused into "teas", or chewed as an appetizer or after-meal digestive. Commercial herbal teas aren't necessary; use a strainer with loose herbs at home. A pinch of kitchen herbs per mug of boiled water is a good rule of thumb. For ginger, three fresh slices per mug, and for star anise, one per person is plenty.

» Green tea, or infusions made from mint, chamomile, chrysanthemum, shiso, or, as mentioned above, ginger

Very often we are presented with appetizers that do not help digestion. While we may be accustomed to them, the items on the chart below do *not* fulfill the role of true appetizers and should not be eaten automatically.

Examples of Poor Appetizers	Why Isn't This a True Appetizer?
Cold Things, Including Iced Water	Digestion only takes place well in a fully warm environment.
Cold or Raw Food	Simply put, cold or raw foods diminish *stomach fire* (digestive strength), making digestion much more difficult.
Bread	Bread is not a true appetizer. It engages the pancreas and spleen functions (carbohydrate digestion) too fully. Bread is not descending, it's too filling, and it's drying. Bread is best as the grain portion of a simple meal, not before eating other things.
Cheese	Cheese is popular and ranges in quality from junk food to artisan creation. But it's not a good appetizer. Cheese is slow to digest and lacks clear directionality. Cheese is best as a snack between meals, if it is in your diet.
Too Much Water	Hydration is essential and too often lacking, but drinking a lot of water along with food dilutes stomach acids and other secretions, making meals harder to digest. Drink plenty of water before meals (20 minutes is sufficient).

Appetizers are not always needed. They are needed for someone whose digestion is less than robust, and will benefit all of us before a large or heavy meal. For example, a well-designed banquet or holiday dinner should include true appetizers to prepare digestion for the meal to come. A sampling of appetizer recipes is included in Book 2. Judge for yourself: start your next holiday dinner with appetizers that meet the criteria described here. When you recall those meals that began with cheese, bread, fried snacks or creamy dips, your own belly will know the wonderful difference true appetizers can make.

Now that we know how to pick starter foods and whet the appetite, it's time to consider the effects that different foods have on the stomach itself.

SIX

Soothing the Stomach and Pancreas-Spleen

The stomach is our digestive gatekeeper, mashing up our (already well-chewed) food, and preparing the mash—known now as *chyme*—for further digestion. When the stomach senses that digestive secretions (acids, enzymes, and so forth) are sufficient, it allows the chyme to progress into the next section of our digestive system. To accomplish its processing role, the stomach likes to be moist and warm. It likes foods that have a natural, gentle sweetness and benefits from foods that stimulate descension. Because it secretes strong acids (this is the *yang* aspect of stomach, as the acids are "hot"), the stomach must continuously replenish its lining (this is the *yin* aspect of stomach). The stomach likes:

> » Moistening foods

> » Gently sweet foods

> » Descending foods

> » Soothing, *yin* nourishing foods

Moistening Foods

The stomach is the body's hub of hydration. For healthy digestion, eating moist foods is even more important than drinking enough water. From the stomach's point of view, the wet foods we eat are time-release doses of hydration. The stomach loves stews, soups, porridges, and steamed grains. Moist foods also support the protective stomach lining. A good diet regulates (balances) *stomach yang* (the acids which stoke appetite and digest food) and *stomach yin* (the lining which protects the stomach from its own acids). Making certain that we eat enough moist foods is absolutely central to our health.

With this in mind, two things are important: choosing hydrating foods and using cooking methods that preserve moistness.

Moistening Stomach Foods (short list)	Rice, millet, corn, whole barley, zucchini, squash, sweet potato
Moistening Cooking Methods	Steaming (grains, vegetables, fish, etc.), boiling, braising (soups, stews, congee, porridge, moist casseroles)

Gentle, Naturally Sweet Foods

In Chinese medicine dietetics, the term *sweet* refers to foods that have a hint of sweetness (and sometimes almost none, but nevertheless are foods that help build us). For early people living in the wild, the sweet taste was a fairly reliable test that a plant, root or berry was not toxic (or not too toxic, in the case of potatoes, for example).

The stomach likes the gentle sweetness of grains and sweet potato. When skillfully used, these foods not only provide some nourishment but directly benefit the stomach itself. They are food medicine to help heal stomach problems. They are true stomach foods.

Note that while gently sweet foods like rice directly benefit digestion, consuming very sweet food will damage digestion and metabolism over time. More on this later.

Foods That Stimulate Descension

Bitter tasting foods are descending (remember olives and artichokes from the appetizer section). Mildly bitter foods help the stomach in its descending function, and extremely bitter foods act as laxatives, strongly stimulating descension and peristalsis (coffee is an example). Descension is essential to welcome food (down into the stomach), avoid reflux (complications arising from rebellious stomach energy incorrectly urging stomach acids upward), and prevent food stagnation.

People today eat fewer bitter foods, often making up the difference with two very bitter foods, even when their bitterness is hidden with sugar: coffee and chocolate. Healthy bitter foods include bitter greens: escarole, chicory lettuce, dandelion greens, radicchio, endive, broccoli rabe, and the favorite in the Chinese community, bitter melon (bitter melon looks like a very wrinkly cucumber).

Root vegetables also are descending. Their nature is to reach downward as they grow; that quality enters us when we eat them to an extent that surprises many modern people (but was obvious in earlier times). Carrots, parsnips, daikon—even when sliced and cooked—are excellent stomach foods, providing descending energy.

Foods That Nourish the Stomach's Lining and Protective Fluids (*Stomach Yin*)

Moistening foods (and wet-cooking methods) that nourish *stomach yin* include:

» Steamed rice, steamed millet, porridges of all kinds (rice congee, millet porridge, oat porridge, corn grits, etc.) These are particularly good for breakfast, or anytime if convalescing.

» Soups and stews

» Zucchini, butternut or other squashes or cooking pumpkins

» Bland, mild foods

In order to support the stomach's lining and protective secretions, it is essential to be aware of foods that overly dry or irritate the stomach. I often recite the following list of stomach irritating foods and drinks when working with individuals suffering from acid reflux, a condition that can be mild or dangerously severe. There are virtually always one or two foods that get an "Aha!" reaction, and sometimes the response is, "That's all I eat!" These foods should be eaten only in moderation by healthy people, and avoided by those suffering from reflux conditions (or the much broader category of *stomach yin* deficiency that can cause symptoms from dry lips to hormonal imbalances).

Foods that irritate the stomach lining and can deplete *stomach yin* include:

» Hot or spicy peppers (cayenne, etc.)

» Other nightshade family vegetables (bell peppers, tomatoes, white potatoes, eggplant)

» Onions and garlic (more on how to use these properly later)

» Coffee

» Alcohol

» Chocolate (a surprise for devotees, but chocolate is very stimulating and can become a problem for many people)

» Carbonated beverages

» Overly drying diet, including overuse of bread and other baked goods

If you love these foods, protect your stomach by not having them too often, and include plenty of the *yin* nourishing foods mentioned just above.

The Stomach and the Pancreas-Spleen

The pancreas-spleen works very closely with the stomach. In Chinese medicine, we say that the pancreas-spleen is the stomach's paired organ.

The *qi* that runs through the pancreas-spleen is in charge of:

» Digestive secretions

» Managing metabolism

» Building and managing blood

» Separating, transforming and transporting nutrients

» Balancing the descension of the stomach with ascending or upholding energy

» Many other important aspects of health

The stomach requires descension to work well, while the pancreas-spleen provides complementary ascending directionality. This is crucial for moving nutrients absorbed through the intestine walls up to the heart and lungs, where they are empowered with breath and the heart's spirit before being circulated to every corner of the body. The stomach breaks down our food; the pancreas-spleen help us metabolize it, ensuring that eating is uplifting.

The other important difference between stomach and pancreas-spleen energetics is that while the stomach likes to be moist, the pancreas-spleen is hurt if there is too much moisture. In other words, if the body is not keeping up with the movement and quality of internal fluids, pancreas-spleen function and digestion gets sluggish and weakens. This condition is called *dampness*, leading to water retention, lethargy, certain weight-gain patterns, and later to potentially dangerous phlegm accumulations. The specific organ of the spleen can today be removed without dire consequences, but the collective functions referred to in Chinese medicine as the role of the pancreas-spleen are absolutely crucial for everyone (even if spleen organ may be missing).

Grains and Tubers Are the Key Foods For Pancreas-Spleen

The gently sweet foods mentioned above as good "stomach foods" are also supportive for the pancreas-spleen. These foods don't taste sweet by modern standards, but when digested well they release a steady supply of blood sugar. If digestion is weak or damaged, the same foods can cause problems. How well we do with grains and carbohydrates is an important indicator of digestive strength. To improve pancreas-spleen function:

> » Avoid refined sugars.

> » Focus on non-glutinous grains: rice, millet, oats, corn, buckwheat, quinoa, amaranth, sorghum, teff.

> » Include sweet potatoes, butternut squash, zucchini, and other gourd-pumpkins.

> » Eat warm, cooked food.

> » Chew food well. (Notice how grains become distinctly sweet tasting when well chewed. Digestion of pancreas-spleen foods often begins in the mouth, if we don't hurry swallowing.)

> » Although non-glutinous grains and sweet potatoes support pancreas-spleen, if digestive function is already weak, even good carbs can cause problems, especially when combined with meats or fish. Therefore, have vegetarian meals regularly, and avoid carbs with meat meals at least some of the time. (See the fuller discussion of carbs and Clear Meals in chapter 9.)

Which Nuts and Seeds Are Best for the Stomach and Pancreas-Spleen?

All nuts and seeds contain protein, fats, fiber and micronutrients, but different nuts and seeds connect more with different organ systems.

The nuts that connect most directly to the stomach and pancreas-spleen are:

> » hazelnuts (filberts) and macadamia nuts (use in moderation)

The seeds that connect most directly with stomach and pancreas-spleen are:

> » sunflower seeds and pumpkin seeds (many varieties of these are available, including pepita)

Is There a Meat That Is a Stomach and Pancreas-Spleen Food?

The pancreas-spleen and stomach connect most directly with grains, tubers and squashes (gourds). Yet, meaningful associations with all the internal organ functions can be made with any of the food groups: grains, meats, vegetables, seeds, nuts, etc. The animal food associated with stomach and pancreas-spleen is chicken. Simply put, grains and other good carbs (sweet potato, butternut squash, etc.) support *stomach yin* (the fluids and lining of the stomach), but chicken supports the *yang* (the warming, transforming) functions of the stomach. To understand how *stomach yin* and *yang* work together, we need to know how the stomach contributes to our immune functions.

The stomach welcomes what we eat and drink. Everything becomes mixed together. We often think of the stomach merely breaking down foods through its strong acids, but just as essential is the way different aspects of the food mix are separated. In classical Chinese medicine, this separation is said to happen under the guidance and energy of the stomach and pancreas-spleen. Special attention is paid to the separation of fluids from the food mix. These fluids are further separated into *thick* or *thin*.

Once separated, these fluids are transported to where they are further processed and utilized. Both aspects are crucial: separating and transporting. Think about a baby nursing on mother's milk—the milk is milky-colored but the baby's saliva, tears and sweat are remarkably clear and pure. This "pure" fluid is crucial for our natural immune defenses. If we are dehydrated, if our stomachs lack the ability to separate pure fluids from our foods and drinks, or if we lack the *qi* to move fluids to where they are needed, we will be vulnerable to common infectious illness that we could otherwise defend against successfully.

> » We need sufficient hydration in food and drink.
>
> » We need to be able to separate fluids from food nutrients.
>
> » We need sufficient energy to move fluids where they are needed (this *yang qi* or moving energy can be low if we are tired or stressed, or if our digestion is overtaxed).

Immunity depends on the stomach having enough hydration and energy to do its work well. Only then can we support the quick-responding capacity to protect from or respond to infections or injuries. This response capacity is a type of *yang qi* called *wei qi* (protective *qi*).

With all this in mind, we can understand how to use chicken best. In earlier times chickens were expensive, a luxury reserved for special family dinners, after which the bones would be made into soup, nothing wasted. Today, people often eat chicken when they don't know what else to eat, as a lighter option to red meat. It's as if chicken simply delivers protein and is devoid of any characteristics, particularly with the trend to remove the skin that holds the bird's fat. But chicken is not a neutral food, it has strong characteristics of its own. It is very warming (inappropriate if a fever is present), and helps internal energy ascend (appropriate for someone exhausted or sick, without a fever). In simple terms, chicken gives the stomach the extra boost it needs to fulfill its functions for immunity.

Since our *wei qi* (immunity, in this context) depends on fluids and *qi*, the best way to eat chicken (to prevent illness or build back strength after a fever has broken) is in soup. Chicken soup provides the energy boost of chicken with plenty of fluids (water and fat), cooked for hours (to make it more easily digestible), along with other stomach and pancreas-spleen foods (root vegetables including carrots), some ascending vegetables (celery, parsley), and kitchen herbs and spices (bay leaf, rosemary, thyme, tarragon, onion, even black pepper if the cold is severe). Used this way, chicken soup helps with building the energy needed to ward off or recover from an illness like common cold or flu. A note of warning: if we have an active fever, that means our bodies are mounting a strong immune defense and we don't need chicken soup (it will add heat to the fire). It is best used when sick with no fever (failing to fight infection) or after a long bout of sickness when we feel weakened (fluids and *qi* are depleted).

Other ways of cooking chicken can also be healthful—roasting, baking, steaming, sautéing, grilling, even perhaps frying—but each cooking method connects with a different organ system. Again, the best method for getting the benefit of chicken for immune support is to make it into soup. More information on the energetics of cooking methods is found in Book 2, along with a recipe for Chicken and Rice Soup.

What Are Good Spices and Kitchen Herbs for the Stomach and Pancreas-Spleen?

Neither the stomach nor the pancreas-spleen work well when cool, so warming spices help digestion (but not hot spices).

» Root or rhizome herbs like ginger and turmeric warm digestion and help relieve bloating, nausea and other distress.

» Seed spices aid digestion of carbs, fats and fatty meats, helping to prevent dampness (sluggish fluids): cumin, cardamom, coriander seed, fennel seed, caraway seed, star anise, and more.

» Cinnamon warms digestion and aids digestion of heavy foods. Cinnamon acts well with breakfast to warm the belly to begin the day. If dinner includes dessert (thus making it relatively heavy), cinnamon is very useful to prevent stagnation (particularly if the dessert includes dairy).

» Leafy kitchen herbs are effective digestive aids and therefore important for stomach and pancreas-spleen, particularly those that are warming and ascending: rosemary, oregano, marjoram. Those that are less warming are still beneficial, including basil, thyme, dill, parsley and cilantro (coriander leaf).

» Scallions are the safest of the onion/garlic group. Garlic and onions are classified as hot and easily irritate the stomach and digestion. Use them sparingly. Scallions can be used freely. Leeks and shallots lie somewhere between.

» Mint is very useful for relieving temporary nausea or stomach upset, including the Asian mint called *shiso* (green or purple varieties). Besides being delicious, shiso is the go-to herb for moderate food poisoning, particularly if the offending food was some type of fish or seafood. Shiso is available fresh in Asian markets and can be dried for storage.

What About Regulating *Stomach Fire*?

Stomach fire is a Chinese medicine term for the active digestive function of the stomach; in modern terms *stomach fire* also includes stomach acid. Too much is as bad as too little. When *stomach fire* is balanced, we can digest even complex meals or comfortably wait to eat (I call this the *pleasant hungry feeling*). When *stomach fire* is low, we lack appetite and easily gain weight when we eat; when too high, heat and agitation can spread beyond the stomach (and we can't gain weight no matter how we may try).

Interestingly, too little *stomach fire* can lead to symptoms of too much (as the stomach upsets itself trying to produce more, disturbing its healthy descending directionality and thus allowing some stomach acid to rise, damaging the esophagus). Many cases of acid reflux begin by stomach acids being too low; symptoms result from overcompensation and directionality problems. In order to have successful resolution of a reflux condition it's important to discern whether it's is due to too much acid or too little (and what role directionality problems have).

Stomach acid is essential for digesting proteins (meat, fish, beans, etc.) but carbohydrates digest only in the *absence* of acids (the enzymes needed for carb digestion only work in alkaline conditions). Digestion is an exquisitely choreographed sequence of functions and responses. The stomach will work with proteins first, then acids are neutralized by internal secretions and carbohydrate digestion begins. With this in mind, it's easy to understand that *stomach fire* (or acid, if you prefer) needs to be well-regulated, rather than artificially increased or decreased.

What is GERD?

Heartburn is now called gastroesophageal reflux disease, *or GERD. Symptoms range from unnoticed to extreme pain mimicking heart attack. The diagnosis of GERD is applied when occasional reflux leads to damage of the esophagus (which at times can be dangerously severe, including damage to the vocal cords and even esophageal cancer). The cause is often said to be a timing malfunction of the lower esophageal sphincter, or LES, allowing stomach secretions to be pushed up into the esophagus, which has little or no protective lining for such strong acids.*

Lists of foods are made to avoid or add, medications are dispensed, but resolution can be elusive. Individuals suffering from GERD sometimes have high stomach acid production, but sometimes acid is very low; sometimes medications to lower stomach acid (prescription or over-the-counter antacids) inadvertently raise acid levels as the body produces more in response to sensing there is suddenly not enough. The suffering can be extreme, prolonged, worrisome and frustrating. Long-term use of antacid medication is not ideal.

Understanding that reflux is fundamentally a problem of directionality provides the key that makes full resolution often simple. Food needs to be on a descending path. The stomach needs to be ready to welcome food, to receive. When the stomach has fulfilled its role, it needs to open only its lower valve (the pyloric sphincter) to allow the partially digested food to descend further.

If the stomach somehow has its energetic directionality disrupted or reversed, we say that it is rebellious, the individual is experiencing rebellious stomach qi. Symptoms can be caught early if seen as a continuum of signs that stomach qi is not descending properly:

» *Appetite seems a bit off. This is an early sign that stomach directionality is not right.*

» *Hiccups and burping are signs that stomach qi is not accepting or welcoming food. For example, people hiccup when having excessive alcohol—the stomach is mildly but demonstrably rejecting it.*

» *Persistent coughing, even if part of a stubborn chest cold, can be a causative factor of reflux as the stomach is upset by the rebellious qi of the lungs (lung qi should also descend, see chapter 13).*

» *Sluggish elimination or chronic constipation means that the entire alimentary canal is slow and not descending properly. Sometimes constipation is caused by rebellious qi of the stomach or lungs not providing proper descending directionality, other times it can cause those problems because the lower center isn't empty to allow descension from above.*

» *Nausea can be mild and nearly constant. In some cases of reflux (rebellious or counterflow stomach qi), nausea can be extreme and vomiting can occur. This should not be confused with bulimia, a rejection of food in a different context, although any repeated vomiting will damage the esophagus and needs to be addressed.*

» *Pain and burning develop (nausea is not always present). Pain symptoms can spread and appear outside what feels to be the digestive tract, for example, in the lungs, throat, chest or heart area.*

Foods to Avoid

Certain foods are best to avoid for anyone with reflux; other offending foods may be personal. Detective work may be required to tailor diets to the individual's needs. In general, however, avoid foods that tend to be disruptive to the descending qi of the stomach, including:

» *Hot spices (cayenne, etc.)*

» *Nightshades (bell peppers-capsicum, tomatoes, eggplant, white potatoes)*

» *Fried foods*

» *Garlic and onions*

» *Coffee and chocolate*

» *Alcohol*

» *Cold and raw foods can upset the stomach. Avoid iced drinks and ice cream, despite the sense that the coldness would be soothing to the acid sensation. Cold stimulates the stomach to increase fire.*

Foods That Help

Include foods that nourish stomach yin and help stomach qi descend: congee, millet, oats, zucchini, sweet potato, butternut squash, carrot (often cooked), olives, artichoke, kale, endive, radicchio, broccoli rabe, dandelion greens, and so forth.

These foods and others like them help restore descension to the stomach. Attention also needs to be paid to strengthening the pancreas-spleen, as that organ system is responsible for keeping fluids in their proper places, in other words, insuring the integrity of the boundaries, throughout the body.

Avoiding trigger foods, clearing constipation or sluggish elimination, strengthening pancreas-spleen and including soothing, descending foods such as those mentioned above will permit healing to take place. In severe cases, the rebellious stomach qi is so habituated that stronger tools are needed. This needs to be assessed individually, but resolution is still very possible, as long as dietary habits are also changed appropriately.

Assessing whether *stomach fire* is in balance may require a well-trained herbalist, acupuncturist or Chinese medicine dietary practitioner. They will look at signs in the pulses, on the tongue, in complexion, ask about appetite, digestion and elimination as well as listen to symptoms that you report. *Stomach fire* is required not only to digest proteins and to assimilate essential minerals and vitamins, but to support a good appetite (not only for food but for life). *Stomach fire* is part of what fuels our desire to go out into the world to explore and experience our own lives in it.

> » To *raise stomach fire*, add small amounts of meat (which requires and therefore stimulates acid secretion), have small amounts of vinegar before eating (one half teaspoon up to two tablespoons), and warming spices (not hot spice). When *stomach fire* is low, eat small well-cooked meals more often. Avoid raw or cold foods.

> » To *reduce stomach fire*, eat less meat, dramatically increase green vegetables (vegetables provide minerals to neutralize acids), add more root vegetables to draw energy down. Add more grains to satisfy the hunger associated with rampant *stomach fire*. Including bitter tasting vegetables is very helpful; these foods are cooling, clearing and descending (radicchio, broccoli rabe, dandelion greens, endive, asparagus, artichoke, olives, bitter melon, chicory lettuce, as well as mung sprouts, snow peas, snap peas, and more). This approach treats excess *stomach fire* with symptoms including reflux, burping, frequent stomach upset, hiccups, nausea, vomiting, and uncontrollable hunger.

A number of very common foods and foodstuffs exacerbate excess *stomach fire*. Reduce these common culprits:

> » Hot peppers, bell peppers, coffee, alcohol, onions, garlic, tomatoes and chocolate

> » Eating with worry, when not hungry, with erratic timing or poorly combined foods will eventually throw the stomach and pancreas-spleen system out of balance.

> » Definitely do have breakfast, but avoid food for two hours or more before sleep. This strongly helps regulate *stomach fire* and pancreas-spleen functions.

Common Problems of Stomach and Digestion

The fundamental role of digestion is to accept nourishment from the world and to transmute food into our own substance and daily energy. This is called *transformation, transportation and assimilation.* When something is wrong with digestion, it affects every part of our complex system. In very simple terms, the stomach receives food and the pancreas-spleen transforms and transports the results all around. This means that problems of digestion are also transported to remote areas of the body.

For digestion itself, common problems are:

- » poor appetite

- » stomach directionality problems (acid reflux, nausea, belching, etc.)

- » tiredness or lethargy after eating

- » food stagnation

- » pain after eating (bloating, distention, pain, gas, urgent need to move bowels, etc.)

- » constipation or diarrhea (sometimes alternating)

- » hemorrhoids

Each issue has specific solutions, intertwined with an individual's health in other organ systems (no single fix or single diet is successful or responsible). Multiple factors must be considered for safety and long-term benefits. That being said, it is very helpful to look at the status of our digestion and how we are helping or hurting it. Be honest with yourself—is your digestion good, or are you perhaps simply accustomed to some common problems? At various times, everyone needs some digestive tuning. At the very least, our diet should shift with the seasons, as we grow and age, and with changing daily needs of busy lifestyles. Digestion cannot be successful if it is ignored.

What Are Simple Things to Do for Stomach and Pancreas-Spleen?

The foods that are good for stomach and pancreas-spleen are foods associated with a rich harvest, golden, full and round, often capable of being stored successfully through the winter. These are called Earth foods, just as our stomach and pancreas-spleen are the organs of the Earth Element in the Five Element system. These foods include:

> » grains (especially all rice types, millet, and corn)
>
> » tubers (potatoes, sweet potatoes, yams, etc.)
>
> » root vegetables (carrots, parsnips, turnips, rutabaga, celeriac, etc.)
>
> » squash or gourds (butternut squash, acorn squash, zucchini, cooking pumpkins, etc.)
>
> » pumpkin seeds and sunflower seeds
>
> » hazelnuts, macadamia nuts
>
> » gently warming spices (rosemary, oregano, ginger, cinnamon, cumin, etc.)

Reducing foods that challenge digestion and adding those that nurture it are the two strongest moves we can make for improving overall health. Sometimes, this change is all that is needed—with improved digestion, natural healing repair can occur from the body's own wisdom. Even when we do require medical help, we will get more benefit from those interventions if we reduce foods that challenge (or even damage) digestion. Our overall health can only improve when digestion itself is improving.

SEVEN

Supporting the Liver and Gallbladder

Earth foods—the foods of the harvest, including grains, squash, tubers and root vegetables—are very supportive of the stomach and pancreas-spleen but are not in themselves a complete diet. We also need protein every day (meat or beans, most simply) and green leafy vegetables. These foods support the Wood Elemental Phase. While Earth Element foods help center us and support basic digestion, protein and fresh leafy greens help us to grow upward and to move. These are the foods that connect most directly with the liver and gallbladder.

The liver has approximately five hundred scientifically identified functions. This could easily be overwhelming, but all those functions fit into three main categories:

» Synthesis of our unique personal proteins, hormones, and other compounds from raw materials provided by digestion of our foods (the liver as "chemical factory")

» Storing blood and nutrients (the "storehouse" aspect)

» Detoxification and clearing (detox)

Chinese medicine also focuses on the idea that since the liver is a storehouse, it must also allow distribution of what it stores (blood, nutrients and the innumerable chemicals it produces). Because this sharing can be smooth or have various problems, the quality of the liver's energetics is very important.

Therefore, foods that are good liver foods are those that help:

» Build and store blood

» Provide protein

» Help clearing and detoxification

» Relax and smooth the "coursing" of *liver qi* (the functional energy of the liver)

Further, there are a number of other associations:

> » Some of the chemicals synthesized by the liver are neuropeptides essential to the nervous system. For this reason, the liver's smooth functioning—or lack of smoothness—contributes to the broad spectrum of our emotional stability and neurological health.

> » As important as the liver's independent functions are, its interactions with the other organs are also very important. The liver has crucial interactions with the organs of digestion (stomach, pancreas-spleen, small intestine), as well as with the lungs, heart, and kidneys.

> » The liver normally supports an ascending directionality. If liver function is overly tight or imbalanced, that ascending tension can overact, leading to headaches, irritability, or high blood pressure. This can be called *liver constraint* or *tightness*.

> » The liver is associated with new growth and the way plants sprout up. Therefore, the liver's energetics are associated with the rising sun, springtime, and, perhaps more importantly for us as we walk through our food markets, with the healthy color of new growth in plants—vibrantly fresh green.

With all this in mind, good foods for the liver begin with:

> » Red meat (especially beef and bison) because it enables our liver to easily synthesize our own proteins and build blood reserves.

> » Green vegetables. Compact vegetables like cabbage or broccoli help the liver in its function of holding or banking blood and available nutrients, while broad leafy vegetables like kale, collard, chard, bok choy, parsley, or some lettuces help the liver in its spreading or smooth coursing of *qi* function. Stalk or stem vegetables support the liver's ascending role, such as asparagus, celery, kohlrabi, or for that matter, the stems of broccoli, kale or parsley. Asparagus is a perfect liver food—it grows straight upward, very quickly in springtime, is green, and has a slightly bitter taste (more on the bitter taste in a moment).

The Liver's Role in Neutralizing Toxins (Detox)

To perform its detoxification function effectively, the liver must have access to an avenue of elimination to excrete those toxins. Otherwise, the liver gets burdened, heavy, eventually swollen or hardened, which is why some people choose to do liver cleanses. (Such cleanses are best done in springtime and with some caution.) The avenues of elimination for the liver are through the blood (naturally, since the liver is very much about blood) and through the gallbladder. Neutralized toxins released into the blood are eventually filtered by the kidneys and excreted through urination; what the gallbladder releases (including retired blood cells) is excreted through the bowels.

The gallbladder is paired with liver just as the pancreas-spleen is paired with the stomach. The liver sends bile to the gallbladder through a major duct system. Bile is held in the gallbladder until the gallbladder is stimulated to release it into the upper part of the small intestine, where it meets the half-processed food (the chyme) coming from the stomach. Because bile is very alkaline and has a detergent-like quality, it can conduct its two principal functions: to neutralize the strong stomach acids that would otherwise damage the small intestine and to help digest fats.

The Role of Bitter Foods

From a food point of view, it's important to know that bile is very bitter. Bitter foods work with the cleansing (detox) aspect of the liver and the gallbladder. As mentioned in the section above on *stomach fire*, bitter foods act to cool excess heat. If the liver becomes overworked by too much red meat with fat (don't forget some fat is essential for health), it can be cooled by bitter green vegetables, including:

- » Chicory, escarole, endive, radicchio
- » Broccoli rabe, Chinese broccoli
- » Olives, artichoke
- » Dandelion greens
- » Bitter melon

Sprouts and Springtime Greens

As mentioned above, one of the characteristics of foods that support liver and gallbladder is that they naturally grow in springtime and tend to grow quickly. Immature or young foods fit that description, especially sprouts from beans, grains or vegetables (often called microgreens). Sprouts strongly help cool and clear liver and gallbladder. Mung bean sprouts are the most traditional, but other bean sprouts and microgreens are easy to grow at home or find in markets (bean sprouts are extremely easy to grow and among the cheapest good eating imaginable). Sprouts are very cooling, in fact, they are often considered too cold. Most people should wilt sprouts by sautéing them for 1 to 5 minutes before adding to a dish.

Wilting Bean Sprouts

Sprouts are very cooling, easily too cold. Digestion doesn't like being cold, but sprouts connect with the liver and gallbladder, organs that are fairly often overheated. Wilting sprouts before eating helps the liver and gallbladder (and therefore blood pressure and emotions) "stay cool" without overcooling the digestive tract.

Rinse two handfuls of mung bean sprouts. Add to a medium hot pan with enough oil to just coat the sprouts. Add sliced scallion, slivered fresh ginger, pinch of salt and a splash of rice wine. Cook until the alcohol is gone, the scallion softens and the sprouts are just wilted, about 3 to 5 minutes depending upon heat. Serve as side dish with any protein, grain, and other vegetables.

Eat 1 to 2 times daily for a week or more to enact a therapeutic change, or just occasionally for basic health maintenance.

The liver also responds well to foods that grow on vines or vine-like bushes. Peas and beans (legumes) are a major source of protein around the world and are also high in healthy oils, vitamins and minerals. These foods grow on vines and are the first crops planted in springtime:

» Peas

» Beans

» String beans, snow peas, sugar snap peas, edamame

Connection with the Nervous System

In herbal medicine, neurological problems have long been treated with plants that grow as vines. In the kitchen this means that peas and beans fit into the liver system. Think of the children's book of the bean plant that grows so fast and tall that it ascends to the clouds and is strong enough for even a giant to use as a scary ladder. Beans grow so dramatically that they are worthy of a classic children's tale—it's only a small leap to imagine them growing overnight with enough energy to reach beyond the normalcy of a country garden or a plate of beans.

Most people today don't grow their own food, and it's easy to forget that peas and beans grow on climbing vines that show enormous vitality. The way herbalists use vines to treat neurological conditions can be understood in a modern context by connecting the liver with neuropeptides and overall neurological functioning. In classical thinking, peas and beans have direct resonance with liver and gallbladder function because they grow on vines that strongly ascend, are green, are the first crops to plant in springtime, and are high in protein and oils. This makes them classic liver foods. Of course, further differentiations can be made: different beans are often used to connect with other organs in addition to liver, based on shape, color and growing characteristics. But first and foremost, beans connect with the liver; when sprouted, beans nourish but also cool and aid detox, connecting particularly with the gallbladder.

Sprouting at Home Is Easy

Any bean or whole grain can be sprouted at home. Simply cover the raw beans with cool water, unrefrigerated, for 8 hours or overnight. On the second day, rinse and drain the beans and let them sit in a bowl covered by a cloth to avoid direct sunlight. Keep the seeds moist but drained to avoid spoilage by sitting in water. Rinse and strain three times daily for several days. Sprouting will start between one and four days, depending on the type of bean. Continue to wash and drain until the desired amount of growth is achieved. Add sprouts to stir-fries or sauté dishes to warm briefly (it's important to warm sprouts to protect digestion from too much cooling). Different sprouted beans can be used for specific purposes, but all sprouts are clearing, cooling, and include that influence on gallbladder and liver.

For grains, it is sufficient to soak overnight, then rinse, strain and cook. Sprouts won't visibly appear, but cooking time will be markedly reduced and their energetics will be much more uplifting and beneficial for digestion.

Fermented Foods Work with the Liver and Gallbladder

On the microscopic level, new growth—spring, at any time of the year—is achieved by fermentation. Fermentation is a kind of rebirth from decay. Tricky, but all cultures have discovered and refined excellent fermentation techniques. Fermented foods stimulate the liver and gallbladder system (or, in the case of alcohol—produced by yeast fermentation—stimulate and then stress that system). Fermented foods are very good for liver and gallbladder, helping their functions and strongly aiding digestion in general. Any food can be fermented:

» Fermented dairy: yogurt, kefir, labneh, sour cream, buttermilk, lassi

» Fermented drinks: kombucha, kvass

» Fully fermented fluids: vinegar (made from grape wine, rice wine, apple cider, etc.)

» Fermented vegetables: sauerkraut, pickles, kimchi (virtually any vegetables can be naturally pickled)

» Fermented soybeans: miso, tamari, tempeh, natto, fermented black beans (other beans can be used, e.g., adzuki miso)

» Fermented fish: South Asian fish sauce, cured salmon or mackerel, etc.

» Fermented grain: sourdough bread, any naturally yeasted product (Some caution is warranted for wheat and other glutinous grains. Yeast consumption can also be a problem for some people with compromised digestion.)

» Fermented grapes, fruits and grain for alcohol (Wine, rice wine, plum wine and distilled spirits have a large place in human culture. Used well, small amounts of wine, rice wine and plum wine are effective appetizers and digestive aids because fermented products aid digestion. For those who do not drink alcohol, including children and those who are ill, the benefits of wine can be included by cooking thoroughly in dishes.)

The connection of fermented foods with liver and gallbladder (even foods that aren't good liver foods unless fermented) highlights another important dietary point: the taste that intrinsically connects with liver and gallbladder is sour. Fermentation produces complex sour flavor notes. Earlier, I mentioned *bitter* as a useful taste that helps to cool and detoxify the liver. But sour is the intrinsic taste that the liver responds to, particularly for its role in storing blood and ready nutrients. Sour helps gather, it astringes.

What Fruits Are Good Liver Foods?

So far, we've looked at several groups of foods that support liver and gallbladder function:

- » Meat for protein and building blood

- » Green vegetables for helping detox (and minerals for enriching blood)

- » Beans for vegetarian protein and liver health (and the idea of vines resonating with liver and gallbladder)

» Sprouts (cooling stress)

» Fermented foods (aiding digestion and the idea of new growth, renewal)

Berries are the fruits that directly connect with the liver energetics, especially in helping the function of building and storing blood. Berries grow on vines or bushes and (although also sweet) have a distinctly tart or sour taste. Farmers are selecting for sweeter and sweeter berries, but only a generation ago, blueberries would be served with sugar on top. Berries are tart, a signature for liver and gallbladder connection.

Many people today are chronically under-rested, overstressed, and have constrained liver function due to excess of one or more of the key liver stressors. Note that some of these are key stressors for stomach, too:

» Alcohol

» Sugar (including hidden sugars and refined carbohydrates)

» Meat (too much protein)

» Fried foods

» Coffee

» Prescription or recreational drugs

Although they have enough blood to bleed or donate at a blood bank, many people are relatively blood deficient, meaning that the liver is not storing and sharing blood in a smooth, well-organized fashion. Women of menstruating age are especially susceptible to relative blood deficiency—even more so if stressed, underfed, and under-rested. A diagnosis of borderline anemia is common, meaning that they do not suffer from anemia as a disease but do have a functional deficiency of blood richness. This can be effectively resolved by diet and lifestyle changes.

Associations of food color are traditionally very important. For example, red beets are a favorite for building blood. If guiding by color is not sufficient, consider that beets are high in iron, potassium, magnesium, and folate, all essential for blood building. Beets also contain micronutrients found to protect arteries from inflammation, lowering risk of heart disease. Some of these compounds have been named after beets: *betanin* and *betalain.*

Like beets, berries are also rich in color and are used to build and manage blood. Grapes are considered as berries that grow on vines. Modern grapes have also been selected to be more sweet than tart, but historically they had just a hint of sweetness. It is helpful to imagine their original tartness so as not to eat too many fresh grapes at one sitting.

Berries and grapes are very helpful foods (as well as delicious). They are important foods to help build blood and especially help the liver store blood.

Once more blood is stored, the smooth coursing of *liver qi* is important so that storage doesn't lead to stagnation. The fruit that helps relax *liver qi,* and in doing so helps the entire mid-region relax is the peel of citrus fruit. Citrus fruit flesh can be quite sweet, too sweet if the liver needs relaxing (remember, symptoms of liver constraint include headaches, most instances of high blood pressure, irritability, some types of insomnia, stress that lingers, and so forth). The peel is just right; not just the zest that cooks often use, but the whole peel including the bitter-sour pith. In herbal medicine we keep various types of dried citrus peel stored for ready use, but fresh peel also works well (use organic fruit, since pesticides stick on the peel).

Because the liver sits just under the ribs and is so close to the breathing diaphragm, anything that relaxes the liver will relax breathing and tightness in the chest. Use citrus peel to relax the chest and open breathing. Use it also to help the liver handle meat dishes that are heavy and fatty, for example the French classic *duck with orange* (peel), or the dish invented by Chinese cooks in America, *orange-flavored beef.* In both dishes it is the peel that is helpful; the orange flesh or juice is too sweet and should not be used.

While peels can aid the digestion of meats, whole fruits should not normally be combined with meats or meat dishes. There are exceptions—certain fruits have been found to pair very well with fatty meats, providing an extra bit of moving energy (*yang qi*) to aid digestion. These "meat tenderizer" fruits are the stone fruits, the drupes or single-seed tree fruits, and can be cooked directly with the meats, along with naturally brewed vinegar:

» Apricot

» Nectarine

» Prune (plum)

» Peach

» Olive

Although not drupes, other fruits used to aid digestion of fatty meats or large meals are cranberries, and especially hawthorn berries (popular among herbalists if not yet chefs and home cooks). These fruits paired with a touch of vinegar provide hints of sweetness and sour together. Today "sweet and sour" sauces are usually a cloying and useless goop made with sugar and food coloring, but skillfully done, a splash of fine vinegar and a few stone fruits cooked with a fatty meat dish not only pleases the palate but supports better digestion of that dish.

What Nuts Connect with the Liver?

Nuts are high in protein and fat, as are beans and red meat (also liver foods). The nuts that are considered to most closely connect with the liver and gallbladder are those highest in fat: brazil nuts and pecans. They are best eaten alone in relatively small amounts, as snacks rather than combined with meals. Walnuts also connect with the liver (as well as other organs) in ways that make them especially valuable. Always check nuts for freshness, discarding any that have become stale or rancid.

Test Nuts for Freshness or Rancidity

Nuts are high in oils, and once shelled they can turn rancid fairly easily. Many people are accustomed to eating rancid nuts, but this should be carefully avoided. Rancid oils are oxidized and therefore damaging to healthy cells. We hear a lot about antioxidants and how they protect us from premature aging and illnesses like cancer; there is no sense adding more oxidized oils to the system.

Buy packaged or bulk nuts at a store that sells a lot of them, never where they seem to sit on the shelf. Put your nose in for a smell as soon as you open the package. If a stale or bitter smell emerges, it is better to throw them away than to eat them. Nuts are great food, but not if turned.

The very best way to eat nuts is to buy them in their shells to eat as you crack them, preferably with a few other people. It's as close to natural human eating as most of us can ever experience.

What Spices and Kitchen Herbs Help the Liver and Gallbladder?

Certain spices can enhance liver energetics, supplementing foods that naturally connect with liver functions or helping to engage liver participation for foods that don't.

Leafy kitchen herbs that grow on upright stalks often connect with liver energetics:

>> Rosemary, parsley, cilantro (coriander leaf), oregano, thyme, dill, etc. (Dill is particularly interesting as a spice for fatty meats and fish high in healthy oils because it stimulates production of bile, necessary for good digestion of fats.)

Seed spices that aid digestion of beans can be considered here, too:

>> Cumin, cardamom, grain of paradise (a cardamom family seed spice), fennel seed

>> Citrus peel (often used as a spice to aid liver's role in digestion, as mentioned above)

>> Root and bark spices (can be used if digestion has cooled) including ginger, turmeric, cinnamon, nutmeg, even clove (classified as very warming or hot)

What's the Short Take on Foods for Liver and Gallbladder?

Liver and gallbladder are crucial contributors for digestion, even though neither organ directly touches our food (as the stomach and intestines do). The liver processes nutrients we assimilate from food, is a storehouse for blood and nourishment, and neutralizes byproducts of digestion and metabolism. Together with the stomach and pancreas-spleen, the liver and gallbladder make up the organs of the middle arena of the torso. The liver and gallbladder work with the stomach and pancreas-spleen to digest and process the basic foods of the human diet: grains, vegetables, meats, beans, seeds, and nuts.

> » The stomach and pancreas-spleen like grains, root vegetables and harvest time foods.

> » The liver likes meats, green leafy vegetables, spring vegetables (e.g., asparagus), compact vegetables (broccoli, cabbage, cauliflower), beans, nuts, fermented foods and sprouted things.

The liver can be overworked by the modern diet, resulting in constraint that in turn leads to tight breathing, high blood pressure, headaches or migraines, irritation, bursts of bad temper, PMS, poor digestion, alternating constipation with diarrhea, and so forth. It's important to avoid the common liver stressors (excess alcohol, sugar, meat, fried foods, coffee, chocolate and if possible, drugs). The liver is also stressed by irregular hours and benefits from fairly consistent eating and sleeping schedules. Foods that help the liver relax include leafy greens, bitter greens, citrus peel, kitchen herbs (like parsley, cilantro, basil, mint, shiso), small amounts of fermented things and sprouts.

EIGHT

Care and Feeding of the Small Intestine

If any major organ is commonly underestimated, it is the small intestine. The liver, heart, lungs, kidneys, even the stomach—these organs enjoy superstar status. People talk often and casually of heart health, liver detox, or lung status, but nobody says, "I'm doing a new program at my gym for small intestine health—it's going great!" or, "I've got takeout for dinner that's labeled small intestine healthy!" We take the small intestine so for granted that we don't even know how to feed it. Let's take a closer look at the work of this unsung organ that lies at the center of digestion and assimilation.

Once the stomach has kneaded our (well-chewed) food sufficiently and senses that enough stomach acid has entered the mash to break down its proteins, the stomach permits the chyme to pass into the upper small intestine. Our food is now under the care of a complex and powerful network of neurons—the enteric brain, sometimes called the *second brain*—about equal in size to the brain of a small mammal. This gut-brain manages all the difficulties we routinely hand it with brilliance, independent of direction from the brain in the head. A separate system is in charge; in today's jargon, the complex intelligence running digestion and assimilation would be called a *smart system*, with the intestine having *smart lining*. Although what we think and feel affects our ability to digest, and what we digest influences what we feel and the clarity of our thought, the enteric brain is beyond our conscious awareness or control. This permits us to digest while doing other things, but also means that it is too easy to ignore what's going on after we eat. We need to learn what we can do to keep digestion healthy and how to correct what might go wrong.

This is a good time to emphasize that the organ names used in the Chinese medicine tradition mean more than just the anatomical organ. In this context, the organ names refer to a collection of specific functions that rely on or pass through the physical organ. For example, when an acupuncturist, herbalist, or dietary specialist says "spleen," they are referring to the way our diet is separated, sorted, mobilized, and metabolized, as well as the way something almost ethereal (the *qi*) is lifted from digestion in the belly and spread upward to chest and outward to the four limbs.

Furthermore, the term *spleen* includes the way parts of blood are made from nutrients, and the way all these factors are directed and held where they need to be. Even for those who have had their spleen organ removed, these functions continue. This idea of collective functioning holds true for all the different organs, each with their specific details. The physical organs are certainly important, but so are the complex and subtle energetic functions that have long been associated with them. Since modern education emphasizes separation of functions, we have to remind ourselves very often of the classical use of organ names meaning *collective function*.

A full understanding of how foods work within us must integrate both views: the mechanical understanding of nutrition as well as the way the specific qualities of foods support or hinder the energetics of our living bodies.

Now we are ready to look at the functions of the small intestine in a new way.

A Note for Clinicians

The small intestine is where many of the functions associated with stomach and pancreas-spleen actually take place. This is a very important point in the context of Chinese medicine, where the focus of digestion is often on the pancreas-spleen, stomach, or liver energetics. Foods must be selected that support those functions within the context of the small intestine. In other words, if the small intestine is weakened (from inappropriate diet, medications, or damage from pesticide residue), efforts to restore the functions of stomach, pancreas-spleen, kidney yang, or large intestine will have a hard time being truly effective. Focus on small intestine health as well as other priorities.

To begin, the small intestine likes many of the same foods that support the stomach and pancreas-spleen:

» Gentle, soothing foods

» Foods that aid descension (and clear food stagnation)

» Meals that digest easily

» Fermented foods

Where the small intestine differs from stomach and pancreas-spleen is in the aspect of "taste" (each organ is associated with a basic taste that stimulates it). The stomach and pancreas-spleen like gently sweet foods, including sweet potato, millet or rice. Those foods also benefit the small intestine, but the small intestine really likes foods that are naturally bitter (my favorites are listed shortly below, on page 71, as descending foods). There are two reasons for this:

» The bitter taste is the taste that stimulates descension of food (and balances ascending *qi* in general). Many people avoid naturally bitter foods, preferring to satisfy the bitter taste with coffee or chocolate (often masked by sugar). The small intestine is indeed stimulated by the bitterness of coffee, but it's better to include some bitter foods in the diet like Italian or Chinese greens.

» Bile—the essential, greenish secretion of the liver that is stored in the gall-bladder until called for by the duodenum—is extremely bitter. The bitterness of bile is necessary to neutralize stomach acids (alkaloid substances are often bitter in taste). Bile is essential for the digestion of fats, and, because bitter exerts a descending influence, it is a natural laxative. Bitter things help move the intestines, clearing food stagnation and stimulating healthy peristalsis. This is not a system we want to ignore. Bitter foods resonate with these functions and make the small intestine happy (yes, there are deep connections between the gut and our psychological well-being).

Here it will be useful to bring more detail into the discussion. To understand what happens to the foods we eat, we need an introduction to the three sections of the small intestine. This will help us better select foods to balance meals for good health.

The small intestine is a very long, winding organ with three distinct sections, each with its own set of specific functions (and different microbial helpers). Here is a simple guide to each section:

» The first section of the small intestine (the *duodenum*) continues functions of the stomach. It has a protective mucosal lining similar to the stomach lining (a continuation of *stomach yin*) to withstand the stomach acids (*stomach yang*) and is the location where proteins are disassembled into amino acids and absorbed (dietary iron is also absorbed here). The duodenum produces hormones in response to the food it senses. These hormones stimulate secretions from the liver, gallbladder and pancreas that steadily neutralize stomach acids and allow successful breakdown of complex food components. The duodenum is about one foot long, sometimes a bit shorter.

» The middle section of the small intestine (the *jejunum*) is the location of many functions dependent upon the pancreas-spleen (as discussed in chapter 6). The jejunum is home to far more microbes than the duodenum and is the location of reabsorption of roughly half of the fluids from the warm, moist chyme. Although this is a function ruled by the stomach in classical Chinese medicine, the place it occurs is below the stomach, in the jejunum. The jejunum is also the location of the digestion and assimilation of most carbohydrates and fats (governed by the energetics of the pancreas-spleen). The second section of the small intestine—2.5 meters or about 8 feet—is therefore the location where harmonization of stomach and pancreas-spleen energetics is crucial, as is good regulation of the liver and gallbladder energetics with the well-tuned stomach and pancreas-spleen. When all this is working well, you're on track for good digestion (just a couple more puzzle pieces needed, like the contributions of the lungs and kidneys).

» The third section of the small intestine (the *ileum*) hosts a different collection of microbes, and is needed for digesting tough starches and other digestive stragglers that didn't yield to either the acids, enzymes or microbes encountered so far. Most digestion and absorption has taken place by now, but not all—the ileum is where vitamin B_{12} is extracted and absorbed, for example. The ileum is the longest section of the small intestine: 3.5 meters or about 11.5 feet. Modern processed food is rich in tasty, easily digested nutrients, so this part of the small intestine (more than half, overall) is underutilized. In early times much of our food would have been difficult to digest, requiring the microbial fermentation that takes place in the ileum. Even with today's diet, the ileum is said to contribute one tenth of our nutrients—extracted by microbes from foods we cannot otherwise digest. More on this a bit later.

How Much Bile Do We Make? How Much Pancreatic Juice?

It's interesting to know that each day we produce about half as much bile as saliva. About the same volume of pancreatic secretions as saliva (between 1 and 2 liters a day!), about the same again for intestinal secretions and stomach juices. Nearly all these fluids are recycled back into our circulation through the walls of the jejunum, ileum and large intestine. Incidentally, all the digestive secretions from saliva to those made in the intestines are alkaline with the exception of gastric acid. Understanding this helps us form a sense of how to balance acid and alkaline in the digestive tract and beyond.

A Lesson from the Classical Masters: The Small Intestine Protects the Heart

In Chinese medicine, the small intestine has very important functions associated with the heart. Beyond its digestive functions, the small intestine is part of the heart's protective team. Think of the heart as the king in chess: all the other players work to protect it. Simply put, the heart suffers when agitation and stress cause too much up-bearing pressure. Excess ascending movement usually underlies high blood pressure or the tightness and pain classically called *chest oppression*. Energetically and mechanically, it is the small intestine that helps protect the heart from excess heat, overly intense internal up-bearing, and the accompanying symptoms of palpitations, pressure and pain. The small intestine clears excess intensity (fire) from the heart, using its descending capacity, its intimate relation to stress hormone production, and its control over internal fluids.

There's no limit to the complexities of the body, but think of it simply: the small intestine is the organ that handles the fiery stomach contents and calmly sorts what is useful from what needs to go. As an assistant to the heart itself, the small intestine energetically helps do the same for our emotions: sort what is important from what doesn't truly pertain to us. If this fails or is overwhelmed, digestive as well as psychological distress can result. The small intestine helps us know what is for us and what is not. When healthy, we can digest not only our meals but all our life experience with strength and leisurely confidence. The small intestine says to the stomach and to the heart, "Don't worry, relax, I've got it." If, that is, the small intestine has its needed resources and is not habitually overworked.

Think About Stress in a New Way

The next time you feel a bit stressed or overwhelmed, try remembering the role of the small intestine. The wisdom of the small intestine is to sort what is for us from what isn't. Let that work on what feels overwhelming. It's calming. We aren't supposed to hold on to problems without sorting them out. In classical terms, this is a function of digestion, and of the small intestine in its role protecting the heart. When we sort properly, we can clear two specific negative emotions: the sense of excess fire (anger) and the buildup of bitterness. Far from ignoring real problems, once we free the oppressive burden of anger and bitterness, we can respond as needed with clarity and compassion.

What Foods Benefit the Small Intestine?

With all this in mind, let's look at foods that are not only digested in the small intestine but actively connect with, support, and benefit the small intestine and its functions.

The small intestine likes:

> » Gentle, soothing foods

> » Foods that aid descension (and clear food stagnation)

> » Meals that digest easily (restoring digestion simply by not overworking it)

> » Fermented foods

For those with compromised digestion, rotating foods is very helpful for two reasons:

> » Rotating foods averts stagnation (for example, having french fries or popcorn daily easily leads to stagnation in digestion).

> » Rotating foods averts unwanted microbial overgrowth of opportunistic yeast, fungi, bacteria, or parasites that favor those repeated foods (for example, having refined sugar everyday can lead to overgrowth of yeasts and other "bad" microbes because their food—simple sugar—is overabundant in the gut).

Gentle foods that soothe the small intestine include:

» Summer squashes (soft gourds with thin, edible skins, including green and yellow zucchini, pattypan, delicata squash, and others)

» Winter squashes, sweet potato, cooking pumpkins (e.g., butternut or acorn squash, hubbard, kabocha, kuri, spaghetti squash, and others)

» White rice, oats, barley, millet

» Foods with gelatinous texture: congee, corn porridge, chia, okra, bone broth, thick soups, seaweeds, gelatins, kanten desserts, kuzu preparations

Foods that aid descension include:

» Root vegetables (cooked carrots, daikon, parsnip, turnip, etc.)

» Bitter greens (The bitter taste is very important for the small intestine in its role draining fire and stress from the heart.) Classical Chinese medicine describes how the small intestine uses its role in fluid management to drain fire through the bladder, a function that often underlies symptoms of UTI or urinary tract infections. In other words, if you've had a UTI that is treated with antibiotics but tends to recur, it probably isn't primarily a bladder infection but inflammation symptoms as the small intestine flushes heat from above down to the bladder, irritating the bladder in the process, sometimes quite dramatically. Meanwhile, the antibiotics tax the good functioning of the small intestine and the microbial world within, often leading to a cycle of what appears to be recurring urinary tract infections. Better to use bitter greens; they are strongly descending and cooling, helping to detoxify via diuresis. Bitter greens include radicchio, endive, dandelion greens, artichoke, olives, spinach, chicory, bitter melon. All work to descend, clear and cool, but they can be differentiated as follows:

  • Olives and artichoke are best for clearing food stagnation.

  • Radicchio and chicory are best for clearing emotions and heart fire.

  • For clearing inflammation underlying UTI, stronger bitters such as dandelion greens and bitter melon are very good.

Descension through the length of the small intestine is conducted by peristalsis, the synchronized waves of contraction/relaxation of the smooth muscle structure of the intestines. Dietary bulk stimulates peristalsis, particularly if high in dietary fiber. High-fiber diets, however, are more difficult to digest, particularly if the small intestine is weak or if the microbiota has been compromised (see page 74 for a note on the microbiota). Dietary fiber requires a lot of microbial processing in the lower small intestine and the large intestine, which means that if the microbial army is weak or imbalanced, distress after high-fiber meals is virtually guaranteed. An artful balance is therefore required.

> » Whole grains provide bulk and fiber and are suited for those not too young, too old, or with weakened digestion.

> » For the young, the elderly and those seeking to restore digestive vitality, softer bulk foods are beneficial (sweet potatoes, white rice, and the foods mentioned above that soothe the small intestine).

> » Millet is especially useful—it is a whole grain, yet it soothes and helps balance the stomach and small intestine.

> » Fruits often contain a good balance of both types of fiber—water-soluble fiber in the flesh of the fruit and non-soluble fiber in the peels. Fruit can be too cooling, however. For improving intestinal function, favor cooked fruits with warming spices (for example prunes, figs, apples, pears stewed with cinnamon, see recipe on page 165 of Book 2).

Resolve Food Stagnation if It Arises

Food stagnation is very common, for some as a chronic condition and for most everyone else on occasion. It's important to notice even mild food stagnation and resolve it if it arises. Food stagnation has a number of overlapping causes:

> » Overeating

> » Eating too late in the day (or erratic eating times in general)

> » Poorly combining foods (Combining foods that digest in distinctly different

ways makes digestion much more difficult, thereby slowing down the process. Slow digestion can lead to problems of food stagnation and internal fermentation. More on this in a moment.)

» Eating while stressed (or eating to sedate emotions)

» Adding food on top of a snack or meal not yet well digested

» Those who dislike vegetables may be lacking clear directionality in their meals, day after day, also leading to food stagnation (and weight gain).

» Simply put, eating a meal that is too difficult for your current digestive strength is likely to cause food stagnation.

Descending foods help clear food stagnation. Seed spices, kitchen herbs, digestive fruits, and sprouts all strongly aid digestion, helping avoid food stagnation before it arises or clear it if it does. Germinated (soaked) whole grains and small beans are important to prevent stagnation by providing fiber and bulk.

» Easy-to-find seed spices that prevent or resolve food stagnation are fennel seed, cumin, caraway, cardamom, coriander seed.

» Familiar leafy kitchen herbs for food stagnation are rosemary, oregano, thyme, marjoram, tarragon, basil, parsley and cilantro/coriander leaf.

» Digestive fruits that specifically aid meat and protein digestion, including prunes, figs, apricots, olives, cranberries and the wonderful-but-underused hawthorn berries.

» Sprouts are excellent for clearing stagnation due to poor digestion of carbohydrates (bread, sandwiches, pasta, pizza, bagels, snacks, sweet baked goods, alcohol, and sugar, refined or otherwise). Fresh sprouts, microgreens, or dried sprouted grains work as food medicine for this common type of stagnation or overindulgence. Cook fresh sprouts briefly to avoid excess cold hurting the stomach and intestines.

» Seeds are also very important to re-establish descension in the intestines and clear food stagnation. Nearly all seeds are descending. Chia seeds are gelatinous and moistening, very good for soothing the small intestine (always have them fully moistened or they will absorb fluids from your digestion). Flax seeds are full of excellent oils and fiber, making them particularly good for stimulating peristalsis and resolving food stagnation accompanied by constipation. Use ground flax seeds for most purposes.

» Whole grains provide fiber, protein, oils, carbohydrates, minerals and vitamins. They add weight and bulk to benefit peristalsis, but only if digestion is relatively strong enough to handle them. Soaking whole grains (1 to 8 hours—any soaking is beneficial) releases sprouting enzymes and profoundly improves the digestibility of the grain once cooked.

» Many people with weak digestion have difficulty tolerating beans. Chinese medicine differentiates between the large beans (more likely to cause bloating, etc.) and small beans (usually okay). The small beans are very helpful for clearing stagnation and stimulating peristalsis (they are high in fiber). Small beans include all types of lentils, split pea, mung and adzuki beans.

What Is the Microbiome or Microbiota?

The microbes that live inside our digestive tract are now seen as a complex and essential inner ecosystem, something like the ecology of an island. The weight of all microbes in a healthy human is said to equal that of our brain, about eight pounds, and over half of that is made of microbes in the digestive tract. At first, scientists called this the "microflora", and although that word is still easy to understand, it was changed to "microbiota" because "flora" sounds like plant life (much of the microbiota is single-cell animal life).

"Microbiome" is often used to describe this environment, but to scientists, that term means the DNA of the microbes within. The modern interest in healthy microbes began with DNA analysis. While sequencing the human genome, huge amounts of non-human DNA were encountered. At first, this DNA was disregarded, considered as a set of anomalies or a result of contamination from the lab environment. But in a stroke of creative thinking, scientists realized that they were seeing a trillion or more microbes, each with their own DNA, living peacefully within us. Since then, we have learned that these microbes are not only tolerated, they are essential to our health. We have co-evolved with them. This radi-

cally redefines each person as a collective of life rather than an individual entity, adding modern detail to what humanity's mystics have long understood. The implications of this are changing medicine rapidly, but will take generations to become intuitive.

Because "microbiome" refers to the DNA of those microbes, the term "microbiota" is preferred for the microbes themselves that reside in each individual. You'll see that term in this book, along with various improvised words I use to help us understand that managing the microbiota is not as daunting as it may seem.

Fermented Foods Aid Digestion and the Small Intestine in Different Ways

In Chinese medicine dietary wisdom, fermented foods are closely associated with the gallbladder. As we've seen, bile is produced by the liver, held in the gallbladder and then released into the upper small intestine following hormonal signals from the small intestine. The small intestine is the beneficiary of the gallbladder's principle function. Because fermented foods stimulate the gallbladder to function well, they also directly benefit the health and function of the small intestine.

Furthermore, healthy digestion includes many specific processes carried out by bacteria and other microbes—we simply can't live without their contributions. If the microbiota is damaged or out of balance, improper fermentation will result inside our gut. Skillfully fermented foods (like yogurt, miso, or sauerkraut) strongly benefit digestion, perhaps by providing some of the necessary end-products of good fermentation and perhaps by reminding our digestion of what good fermentation is like. Think of milk that has had yogurt culture introduced to it. Transformed into yogurt, milk can last much longer without spoiling. On the other hand, if the wrong microbes reach the milk, it simply spoils and is soon unfit for consumption. "Good" microbes create complex flavors, preserve foods, and strongly aid not only the liver and gallbladder but the small intestine as well.

Fermentation makes food easier to digest and strengthens digestion overall, but it doesn't completely change the nature of the original food. Sourdough bread is easier to digest because the fermentation predigests the wheat, but those sensitive to wheat may still suffer from eating it. Miso from China or Japan is a very safe way to eat soybeans, but those allergic to soy will still need to avoid it. Further, fermented foods—natto is a good example—can be strong-smelling and an acquired taste.

The variety of fermented food available today offers benefits from different foods and different microbes. Differences are important—for example, fermented dairy is not the same as fermented vegetables. Every culture relies on a specific set of characteristic fermented foods. It's good to begin with the fermented foods of your own culture. Then, explore the wealth of fermented goodies from around the world available today. What we use regularly (and often make at home) include:

» Yogurt, kefir, buttermilk (easy to make at home, we sometimes do)

» Dill pickles (easy to make at home, we sometimes do)

» Sauerkraut (easy to make at home, we sometimes do)

» Vinegar (easy to make at home, but we don't)

» Kombucha (supremely easy to make at home)

» Miso (possible to make at home)

» Naturally brewed tamari (also possible, but we don't make at home)

» Kimchi (easy to make at home, but be careful of the hot spice and garlic, too much can ruin the benefit for many people)

» Natto and tempeh (we don't make at home)

» Fermented black beans (find in Chinatown markets, good natural markets, or online)

» Szechuan pickled vegetables (find in Chinatown markets, or use kimchi or sauerkraut—different but related)

» Many other fermenting ideas can be found from the growing home-fermenting movement in books or online (including homemade wine and beer that can be useful in cooking). Feel free to adapt recipes. It is very common for fermented food recipes to ask for too much garlic or hot spices; it's best to reduce those to a hint or simply leave them out. On the other hand, fermenting is just about the only time I use sugar—the microbes feed on the sugar leaving a pleasantly complex sour taste in its place (homemade kombucha is an example of this).

Eat fermented foods in small amounts—a little bit introduces enough of their influence. Recently a very intense woman came for her session and announced that she's finally stopped drinking beer and wine (she had been a champion consumer) and was excited to tell me that the café below my office sells kombucha from huge vats, that you could get a pint at a time to chug. As a transition from alcohol abuse this is okay, but kombucha functions best in small amounts, 1-2 ounces (30-60 ml, basically a shot glass or two) before meals.

As mentioned, cultured foods retain some of the energetic signature they had before fermentation. Therefore, you can choose a fermented food to stimulate gallbladder and benefit small intestine digestion (all fermented foods do that), and then refine your choice by selecting *which* fermented food based on its original food energetic connection. For example, black soybeans connect strongly with the kidneys. Either freshly cooked or canned, black soybeans are used as a normal bean to satisfy hunger, provide nutrients, support kidney and liver strength, and make delicious dishes. But when fermented, black soybeans are eaten only as a condiment, usually in *black bean sauce*, familiar from Chinese restaurants (it's wonderful and easy to make at home, too, see recipe on page 223 of Book 2). It is now their fermented flavor and health influence we want—and while they still contribute nutrients, we're not eating them as a principal component of the dish, but as a condiment (albeit an important one). Fermented foods should be used in this way.

Fermented foods can be eaten as an occasional appetizer for specific use—to clear mild food stagnation, for example. To get deeper benefit for the small intestine and for supporting the rebuild of the microbiota, it's necessary to include cultured foods steadily and regularly (similar to using probiotics). The way miso soup is used in Japanese cuisine is a good example—it appears daily, and can easily be had at breakfast, lunch and dinner, in restaurants or homes. In general, traditional use of fermented foods is advised, following customs of the cuisines that developed them.

Fermented Foods Are Not the Same as Food Fermenting in Our Belly

When food sits undigested, "bad" microbes go to work, causing symptoms of dysbiosis: bloating, gas, distention, pain, allergic sensitivities, diarrhea or constipation. Toxins can leak into the blood, arousing inflammation of many types throughout the body. This is entirely different from eating well-fermented foods. These foods do not add to this condition, rather, they actively protect from it and gradually help clear it by introducing helpful microbes to the gut.

An axiom of Chinese dietary medicine states that it's more important to have good digestion (even with poor food) than great food with poor digestion. But if we do find ourselves with digestive weakness or distress, we need a comprehensive strategy that helps us feel better in both short and long term. Although there is much more to know, we already have enough information to begin an effective and responsible healing approach to improve digestion. And of course, this approach must be easy to understand and individually adaptable. This healing strategy is based on eating *clear meals*, a term I use with clients and students to describe the way of eating that works for a given individual. We'll learn more about this extraordinarily powerful tool for self-healing in the next chapter.

NINE

Digesting with Ease: Clear Meals

Although the term *clear meal* doesn't appear in scientific papers or classical texts, it is a term I use often in dietary consults to describe a feeling where meals digest well and fully, in other words, clearly. Learn what that feeling is, even if it has been years since you have felt it. It's simple, it's effective, and it's more than safe. The benefits begin quickly and grow over time. I'm often asked how long it will take to notice improvement with dietary changes, but I don't have to tell people what I think, they feel it themselves after the first meal or two.

Clear meals are meals that can be digested well and in a timely fashion. Clear meals are personal because each person's digestive vitality is unique, and also changeable, based on varying factors (amount of sleep, past dietary habits, illness and age are some examples). My dietary clients are familiar with the simple idea of the clear meal:

> **Eat according to what you can digest well, no more.**

It's not just a list of foods; combinations are also very important, as described below. Often, no other self-discipline is needed. Eat personal clear meals, and many long-standing health problems will begin to disappear. Without the continued cause of overworked digestion, poor health improves naturally, often dramatically. This is such an important idea that it deserves a closer look.

Clear Meals Make the Small Intestine's Job Simpler

Digestion is complex. Efficient digestion is well-timed, well-synchronized, and thorough. When digestion isn't strong, all the organs suffer. Toxins can enter the bloodstream and lymphatic system; inflammation results. Health slowly degenerates. Simplifying digestion is a powerful method to start healing at the root of the matter. Clear meals are composed of foods and food combinations that digest efficiently for you. They allow the small intestine to *rest as it works*.

As omnivores, humans have an impressive capacity for mixed eating, but the modern diet and stressful living are eventually too much for many people; their digestion slows and weakens. More digestive taxation can inadvertently be caused by common modern medicines (digestive restoration should be standard after many—or perhaps any—drug treatment, especially antibiotics, but also aspirin and other over-the-counter pain medications). When digestion is weakened, the complex digestive choreography of secretions and food transport is no longer efficient. Fermentation by "bad" microbes takes place when food is in the warm, moist belly without effective or efficient digestion taking place. This is food stagnation, experienced as:

» Lethargy after eating (the strong desire for a nap, sugar or caffeine after a meal)

» Brain fog (feeling of mental fatigue and difficulty with focus)

» Bloating, distention, abdominal pain, gassiness

» Urgent diarrhea or constipation

The details vary for individuals and treatment will naturally vary as well. The principles that are common, however, are:

» *Those with digestive issues will benefit from simplified meals that can be digested efficiently* (improvement will be seen even with health problems that seem unrelated to diet).

» *Clear meals will vary depending on the individual's strengths and weaknesses, changing over time.* Therefore, a home cook is well-advised to master a range of meals from extremely soothing and simple (congee, and separating carbs from proteins, for example) to more complex combinations of whole grains, vegetables and proteins. Then you're ready to "turn the dial", fine-tuning meals on the scale of soothing to challenging with variety and finesse.

Defining Basic and Therapeutic Eating

As with all things, focused intention is key. Dietary intention can be divided into three very broad divisions:

» *Eating whatever I may desire (standard American diet, or SAD)*

» *Eating to be health-supportive in general ways (basic eating)*

» *Eating specifically to improve or resolve conditions (therapeutic diet, including clear meals)*

This book and the recipes in Book 2 focus primarily on basic eating. Focusing on clear meals offers a safe and easy entry into therapeutic eating. Both basic health-supportive eating and therapeutic diet help clear damage done by SAD (which could be known as Standard Poor Eating Habits, SPEH).

What Is a Clear Meal for You?

Here are some basic guidelines:

» *Eat smaller meals or wait longer between meals, to allow full digestion.* Eating more food on top of food not yet well-digested is a recipe for trouble down the road.

» *Snacking should be avoided unless truly hungry.* Most snacking is habitual, emotionally driven, or in response to low blood sugar levels resulting from poor digestion. Especially for adults, snacking is a blood sugar short fix; eventually we need to repair the root of the problem. Good snacks are like good appetizers—they actively improve digestion rather than subdue vague emotional desires or mask blood sugar regulation problems. Healthy snacks contribute to personal health. More on snacking and *snack damage* just below.

» *Reduce or eliminate sugar, including honey, maple syrup, etc.* Readily available sugar—whether refined white sugar or "natural" sugars—provides such easy blood sugar that the digestive process stops the more difficult task of extracting sugars from carbohydrates such as whole grains, tubers, refined grains, breads or pasta. Having quickly satisfied the need for restored blood sugar levels from the sugar, digestion slows, allowing carbohydrates to ferment. Eliminating sugar (added or hidden) tells the body to derive blood sugar from digesting more complex foods. Natural sugars such as honey are not a free pass to have sugar without damage.

» *Separate proteins and carbs, eat fruits alone, eat dairy (including cheese) alone if at all.* We are omnivores, and when healthy we can digest proteins and carbohydrates combined in one meal. For example, a sandwich, meat and potatoes, or rice with fish. These combinations help us feel full for a long time precisely because they digest so slowly when eaten together. Eat a farmer's breakfast before a long day if you want to stay feeling full longer (if you have a robust farmer's digestion, that is). But, for the same reason, these combinations are too much for those who are stressed, sleep deprived, or have weakened digestion. If digestion is less robust, these food combinations are impossible to digest well. It can't be said too often: what digests well for some can be too difficult for others (or for the same person at different times). Healthy choices are deeply individual. Learning how to separate proteins, carbohydrates and dairy into easily digested meals is a very powerful tool for health. If lunch has bread or rice and no animal food, dinner can have fish or meat and no carbs. Dairy is best eaten alone if at all. Fruit is best eaten alone, as a snack (there are some skillful exceptions). Green vegetables and most root vegetables combine well with either protein or carb meals. Using this method, complete nourishment is achieved each day, but not in each meal. Digestion is far more efficient using this method.

» *Avoid cold drinks and raw food—cold and raw slows digestion.* Some people can handle cold and raw food, of course, but if digestion isn't very robust, the taxation from cold drinks and raw food can lead to undigested food in the stool, diarrhea, or inflammation, as the body raises too much heat in response to taking in cold or raw food and drink when already weak internally.

» *Discover food stagnation (if present) and steadily resolve it.* Simple methods to resolve food stagnation are explained in the next two points about directionality and healthy elimination.

» *Use green vegetables, root vegetables, kitchen herbs and spices to provide clear directionality to meals.* This means that rather than a meal sitting heavily in the belly, meals with more vegetables and herb spices help the body sort and transport the components of the foods as they digest. Most vegetables and all spices have clear directional signals for the body, for example, asparagus *lifts*, kale and collard greens *spread* out, carrots *descend* (potatoes, squash and tubers soothe digestion but are not useful for moving directionality—they support the *center*). Many people who are overweight with food stagnation prefer centering foods while habitually avoiding vegetables with clear directionality (celery, carrots, asparagus, kale, chard, artichoke, broccoli rabe, mustard greens, etc.) and kitchen herbs (rosemary, oregano, basil, thyme, parsley, cilantro, ginger, scallion, chives, and so forth). Specific directional foods can be selected with more training, but *any* directional foods can help clear food stagnation.

» *Remember, everything works together.* For many people, food stagnation is accompanied by constipation. When chronic constipation is present, meals will digest poorly and food stagnation (along with bloating, distention, and abdominal pain) is common. This is a serious matter that needs to be resolved, often gradually. In order for appetite, digestion, and metabolism to work well, the bowels must not be sluggish or blocked. More on this subject further on.

Working with these guidelines, you will discover what makes a clear meal for you. Keep in mind:

» A clear meal is nourishing and digests fully within 2 to 6 hours.

» If digestion is too slow or stalls, internal fermentation and accumulated toxins can arise.

» If digestion and elimination are too quick, however, malabsorption of nutrients can result.

» Clear meals vary according to the individual and as health changes.

» Simplifying meals, separating carbs-proteins-dairy-fruit as mentioned above, and avoiding adding simple sugars in dessert are powerful tools to improve digestion and allow digestion and metabolism to recover.

Clear Meals Are Not Strict Meals

Sometimes in my private sessions, when I say "clear meal", I notice that the client writes down "clean meal". "Clean" is good, but the idea of a clear meal is not judgmental or even about "healthy" foods. It's about an enjoyable meal that digests well and fully, leaving you feeling better than you felt before. Most kids have good digestion, and that's a model for us: they race around spending tons of energy, get tired, have a snack and start racing around again, restored by the snack or meal rather than feeling lethargic after eating. That's what food is for, to restore us.

A clear meal is not a judgment on other food. It's a way of paying attention to what our digestion can handle. Through this process, we allow our digestion to improve, enabling us to live longer lives with more vitality.

Avoid *Snack Damage*

Snacks or desserts can ruin successful digestion of an otherwise good meal. It's a shame to spend the effort to eat well, only to spoil everything with a poorly conceived dessert or by having a snack too soon afterward. Snacking should not be habitual; try snacking with the intention to add to health rather than challenge it.

> » A good snack is one that doesn't interfere with digestion or damage metabolism.
>
> » Snacks should be easy to digest so they won't sabotage the next meal.
>
> » Good snacks are often *true appetizers* that can help digestion of the next meal (see recipes for true appetizers in chapter 2 of Book 2).

Take a look at your snacking habits. Do you snack because you feel tired or need some quick sugar for energy? If so, digestion is inefficient and needs improvement. Is it from boredom or frustration? Or are you struggling to steady blood sugar to stave off headaches and mental fog? Or perhaps is it because *stomach fire* is excessive, making you feel constantly hungry? Looking at your snack habits can provide important information on how your digestion may need to be fundamentally improved.

Look at Your Habits

Looking into our habits (including cravings and aversions) is very important, a powerful way to move our lives forward. What foods do you rely on when stressed? Is there a food that you feel a meal is incomplete without, such as potato, rice, meat, or dairy? Do you have a habit of very hot-spicy food? Do you habitually skip breakfast, eat late at night, insist on iced drinks even in cold weather, or find yourself with any one food or drink nearly every day? Healing is about change. Look at your habits. Our repetitive diets actively lock us into our health status and even our character traits. Choose what direction you'd like to move in by looking at your habits and making some changes, even if they are at first small.

Good snacks can be nuts, dried fruits (combine to make homemade trail mixes), grain crackers, fresh fruit, even cheese. (Cheese causes problems for many people, but if it's in your diet, the best way to eat it is between meals, as a snack.)

Vegetarian Eating Can Be Helpful, But Not Always

Because grains (carbs) and proteins (often animal food) digest with very different secretions and therefore with different timing, vegetarian eating naturally simplifies digestion. Most people would benefit from more vegetarian meals or all-vegetarian periods, for a variety of reasons. From the clear meal point of view, avoiding meat and fish means that the synchronization of digestive secretions is less complicated. This will help make clear meals without further effort.

However, there are other factors that need to be considered. First, some vegetarians eat cheese, and for many people cheese is difficult to digest and easily adds phlegm to the lymphatic system. (If you do eat cheese, select high-quality, well-produced cheeses, along with the use of spices such as oregano, rosemary, tarragon, sage, or caraway, cardamom, cumin, etc., to help "cut" through the thickness of cheese for digestion.) From a health point of view, a diet that avoids dairy but includes fish or meat is much easier to digest for many people (leaving broad ethical consider-ations aside for the current discussion).

Without dairy, a vegan must be very deliberate about consuming enough protein, and this main-ly comes from beans combined with grains, nuts and seeds ("legumes" or "pulses" are more elegant names for beans). This works well only if digestion is strong enough to efficiently digest beans. If digestion is weak, first try the small beans (lentils, adzuki, mung) and if those still cause bloating or discomfort, try tofu (tofu includes high-quality protein but has had all the fiber removed, see the recipes in Book 2 for more discussion of tofu). Include soups, mushrooms, sea-weeds, non-glutinous grains, root vegetables (in soup if digestion is very weak), fermented foods, green vegetables of various characters, nuts and seeds if possible, and fruits (dried or stewed if internal cold is present, fairly common in vegans). This can easily be a broad enough diet to support health, but remember that a poorly balanced vegetarian diet is not a healthy one. Sugar can still be a serious problem, potentially even more so for those who avoid the strong energetic influence provided by animal food. Without animal food the diet naturally is weighted more on the carbohydrate (plant) side of the spectrum, and sweets are, of course, very concentrated refined carbohydrates.

Be mindful of these three potential pitfalls of the vegetarian diet:

> » *Cold* can accumulate in digestion and beyond (manifesting with symptoms as varied as a chronically runny nose, undigested food in the stool, or borderline anemia due to digestion being too cool to assimilate dietary iron).

> » There is a risk of falling behind in protein consumption for vegetarians who avoid beans due to problems digesting them.

> » Vegetarianism must not be simply a meatless standard modern diet filled with junk food, sweets, and overly refined carbs.

If digestive problems develop for vegans or vegetarians, separating animal food from grains or other carbs isn't pertinent but restoring digestion still is. (Beans, nuts, and seeds are all vegetarian foods, and the importance of combining beans with grains to ensure complete protein takes priority over separating protein and carbs into different meals.) For vegetarians to improve digestion, first remove any junk food, processed food, or sweets, then look to see if warming spices are needed to restore *stomach fire* (often low in vegetarians because stomach acid is stimulated by being needed to digest meats). Mild anemia is a common sign of low *stomach fire* (dietary iron requires robust stomach acids to be assimilated). Gradually increase whole foods and their fiber. The path of healing will be somewhat different from meat-eaters, but remember, every individual needs an individual assessment to truly understand what is going on. In the clinic, there are always surprises.

Work on Achieving Digestive Clarity

No one admires everything that happens on the desk of every American president, but one thing that is consistently admirable is that all paperwork is traditionally completed, cleared and filed at the end of each day—the presidential desk doesn't allow work to carry over unfinished. Each evening the desk looks new, ready for whatever may come next.

Ideally, our digestions should enjoy that renewed clarity as well. This is the meaning of breakfast, after all—to reintroduce food to a clear belly as we begin a new day. Dinner was good and digested fully through the evening. If we digest through the night, digestion never gets a rest (and we can't possibly wake well-rested). Simply put, digestion should start, work well, and finish, in order to enjoy its own rest time. Being able to feel well through periods of non-eating (at least a few hours between meals and through a full night) is a very good sign of strong physical and emotional health.

If someone can eat a banquet and digest it fully before sleep, then they do not need the guidelines for simplified clear meals in this section. Not everyone needs to separate foods to improve digestion, but for those who do, applying these principles makes a huge difference. Basic eating remains combining grains, greens, and some protein, but for those who wish to really improve their digestion, whether for losing weight, resolving abdominal problems or problems that appear distant from digestion such as autoimmune illness or inflammatory conditions, the idea of a clear meal is important. Again, a clear meal is whatever digests fully and efficiently for your state of digestive strength. Simplify one step at a time to find your clear meal guidelines:

» Separate desserts from mealtime—sweets interfere with digestion of complex carbs and proteins.

» Wait for snacks until you are genuinely hungry, or simply wait for the next meal.

» Eat more directional foods: green vegetables, carrots, seed spices and kitchen herbs (not hot spices, though).

» If needed, resolve chronic constipation (further discussion in chapters 15 and 16).

» As needed, separate carbs from proteins and have dairy as well as fruit alone. Carb and protein meals can both have plenty of green vegetables (but treat potatoes as a starch, like rice, not as a vegetable like broccoli). For example, have a burger with no bun or fries, but with a salad or cooked string beans. Later, have the carb meal, perhaps rice, beans and broccoli, or maybe string beans with baked sweet potato and butter (or olive oil). Oils and seasonings can be included with proteins or carbs. Separating carbs and proteins is very powerful and allows digestion to heal because we are digesting things that work easily together. Try separating carbs and proteins for a few weeks to explore the difference. Once feeling better, separating these food groups can be either a consistent or occasional practice.

» Finish eating at least two hours before sleep (more if the meal is complex). Sleep should be restful for our digestion too.

Clear meals are the entry point into therapeutic diet. Nothing specific is required at this point beyond avoiding combinations of foods that are difficult for you to digest together. This can be a lifestyle (why would we want to eat what we can't digest?) or temporary. The main two points are these:

» *What is most important is not the foods we choose but our ability to digest them well.* Poor food digested well is preferable to very good food digested poorly. Focus on digestion more than the reputation of foods (although of course quality food with good digestion is best).

» *Eating appropriately for your personal health can be delicious and satisfying.* It feels good to feel good. If you want a favorite food, have it in a way that you can handle, even if that means alone, between meals as a snack. But mostly, eat what you can digest well, and learn to recognize the warm hum of the belly when it is successfully digesting a custom-made meal.

TEN

Healing the Small Intestine:
Foods to Relieve Inflammation, Cold, and
Leaky Gut Syndrome

Eating clear meals (at home or when eating out) can be of enormous benefit to maintain or restore good digestion. Beyond those fundamentals, however, there are many specific issues that can arise in the small intestine that warrant special attention. Learning to recognize and solve these problems adds depth to cooking wisdom for everyone, whether or not they suffer with these issues themselves.

You'll recall that the small intestine:

» Continues the work of the stomach (especially in the duodenum section, working on proteins and foods requiring strong acids to digest).

» Continues the work of the pancreas and spleen (secreting enzymes that regulate metabolism and the digestion of carbs and oils).

Foods that help restore those functions were discussed briefly in the chapters on stomach, pancreas-spleen and digestion. Those foods can also be used to help the small intestine, especially when eaten as part of clear meals.

Remember, when you are eating clear meals you can still have the foods you want, just not all mixed together (and not too much of them). Even if you crave something that you know is not good for you, now you know that if you have it alone—as a snack—it won't set you back as far as it would if you laid it on top of a full meal.

Imbalances of the stomach, pancreas-spleen, liver and gallbladder will all impact small intestine. The traditional approach in Chinese medicine is to treat any digestive problems first through treating stomach, pancreas-spleen, liver and gallbladder. This makes a lot of sense because using foods that help balance those organs will contribute strongly to small intestine health as well.

But today we are confronted with modern intestinal damage due to the use of antibiotics and NSAIDs (non-steroidal anti-inflammatory drugs such as Advil, Aleve, and others; see more on pages 98-99). We've also seen a vast increase in sugar consumption in modern times. These drugs (especially antibiotics) can decimate our healthy intestinal microbes, and the excessive use of sugar allows bad players to take over and colonize in the wrong places. Let's look at some of the problems specific to the small intestine, and consider what foods can help sort things out.

Heat in the Small Intestine (Including Urinary Tract Infections)

Heat or inflammation in the small intestine produces physical and emotional symptoms including distention, excessive intestinal rumbling, pressure or an oppressive feeling in the chest, difficulty urinating (including UTI), restless sleep, and agitation. It also can lead to difficulty sorting out what the emotional heart really wants or truly identifies with (loss of better judgment or emotional anchor). Since the small intestine *handles* excess heat in the body, it can be subject to problems *from* that heat as it works to clear it. This can lead to conditions of either dry-type constipation (the heat dries the stool) or explosive diarrhea and conditions defined in Western medicine as irritable bowel syndrome (IBS) or Crohn's disease. Foods that help clear heat (or inflammation) in the small intestine include:

» Soothing small intestine foods mentioned earlier, including sweet potato, zucchini, white rice, congee, oats, barley, okra, string beans, seaweed, and vegetable broths.

» Foods that stimulate secretion of bile. Bile is bitter, clearing and cooling. Use dill, rosemary, asparagus, artichoke, celery, grapefruit, lemon, carrot, dandelion greens and radish to stimulate helpful secretion of bile.

» Sprouts, because they are cooling. Use bean sprouts, microgreens of alfalfa, broccoli, kale, daikon, etc., and grain sprouts, primarily barley sprouts, rice sprouts, and sprouts of antique wheats.

Cold in the Small Intestine

Cold can settle into the digestive tract in various ways, leading to pain that feels dull, often with excessive rumbling (called *borborygmus*) and watery diarrhea. Urinary difficulty can result from cold in the intestines as well as from heat. (See box text on page 92 for a summary of signs and symptoms of *hot* or *cold* type urinary difficulties.) Dietarily, cold needs to be *scattered* by warming herbs made into infusions or cooked into dishes. We've mentioned some of these herbs and spices in earlier chapters, but it's always helpful to review in a new context:

» Fresh ginger (warming), dried ginger (so warming it's considered *hot*), and turmeric powder help warm the belly, the intestines, and thus the bladder. Use ginger in dishes or in fresh ginger tea. (To make a ginger tea infusion, steep three slices from a fresh ginger root in hot water, sip when cool enough to be comfortable.)

» Seed spices can also be warming and very helpful (cumin, fennel seed, caraway, cardamom, coriander, mustard seed, grain of paradise, black pepper, star anise).

» There are quite a number of types of cinnamon that can be used; each are warming although in slightly different ways. Even more warming than cinnamon are cloves. Cloves are considered hot, so be careful not to overuse. Cinnamon, cloves, nutmeg, turmeric, ginger root, cardamom, even black pepper and a number of other spices are so effective in warming internal cold and supporting stressed digestion that they are used in herbal medicine as well as within cuisine. Success depends on properly differentiating internal heat conditions from internal cold (of course, each type of each herb can skillfully be used in surprisingly different ways, but for now they can all be used to warm exhausted digestion that has gathered cold). Pay attention to signs of good progress or of having used too much, adjusting appropriately.

» Most leaf kitchen herbs are warming and help scatter cold (rosemary, oregano, cilantro, tarragon, etc.)

» More important than adding special foods is avoiding cold in the diet. It is essential to avoid iced drinks, raw foods (including salads), juices, ice cream, and too much raw fruit. Even sprouts should be warmed (wilted) on the stove. Although some enzymes and nutrients will be lost, they still strongly aid digestion and it's important to warm up the inherent cooling quality of sprouts.

Urinary Difficulties Can Result from Heat or Cold in the Small Intestine

Heat type urinary difficulties include:

> » *Inflammation*
> » *Burning sensation*
> » *Urgency*
> » *Dark-colored and strong-smelling urine*
> » *Sometimes a diagnosis of UTI*

Cold type urinary difficulties include:

> » *Insufficient emptying of the bladder even though you know and feel you need to release more (this is scanty urination)*
> » *Clear and nearly scentless urine*

Note: This is about heat in the small intestine; sometimes heat arises just outside the small intestine walls. That is discussed later in this chapter, in the section on leaky gut syndrome.

Food Stagnation in the Intestines

Food stagnation can occur anywhere in the alimentary canal, but usually strikes in the stomach or intestines. Stagnation occurs when foods move too slowly through the digestive process. Use root vegetables and whole grains to descend. Bitter greens are also descending, but don't use them too much if internal cold is present because bitter can also be cooling. Spices are very important to ensure movement (use the spices for food stagnation: fennel seed, cumin, cardamom, ginger, and others.) Cooked leafy vegetables also are very important for the strong directionality that they provide. Mustard greens, for example, could work well here, being bitter but also spicy, helping to move stagnation.

It is just as important to avoid the three main sticky food groups—sugar, dairy, modern wheat—which tend to hold things in place.

Food stagnation can arise from many causes:

> » Cold in the pancreas-spleen slows transformation and transportation of the meal.
>
> » Fatigue affects the pancreas-spleen, reducing digestive strength.

» Because the kidneys and adrenal glands support digestion in essential ways, adrenal fatigue undermines good digestion (more on this in a moment).

» Blood deficiency slows digestion as the liver tightens in an attempt to hold what blood it can, exerting a constraining effect on the smooth flow of *qi* throughout the body.

» Overeating naturally slows digestion.

» Even good foods in poor combination can slow or nearly halt digestive progress.

» Certain foods very easily cause food stagnation (popcorn, too much refined food, deep-fried things).

» Emotional stress slows digestion. Stress hormones move blood from digestion to muscles and sense organs in case emergency responses are needed. We can only digest well when we are relaxed.

» Hidden psychological issues of resistance or rejection can deeply interfere with digestion, including causing food stagnation.

When working to change health, resistance often arises ("Life isn't worth living without my chocolate in the evening!"). To ease resistance, make small commitments ("I'll experiment with having no chocolate for two weeks, but if I don't notice anything, I'm going to eat tons of it!"). Small commitments that can be achieved will add up to very significant changes if sustained. It's important to know your character type. Some people need time to make changes, others are eager to change drastically as soon as they hear what may help. Work in a way suited for your character.

Leaky Gut Syndrome

We've talked about heat *within* the small intestine, but when particles not fully digested leak through the membranes of the small intestine wall, the immune system is roused to contain and clear them, causing an inflamed state *outside* the walls of the small intestine. Once they have moved through the membranes of the small intestine, these substances are circulated in the blood and the lymphatic system, creating some degree of inflammation wherever they go.

Normally, only very small, fully digested particles are allowed passage into the blood and lymph systems. When digestion is working well, these minute particles are no longer food, they are fully broken-down nutrients. They are no longer chicken, rice, or olive oil, they are only amino acids, simple carbohydrates (called *monosaccharides*) and the end product of lipid digestion (called fatty acids and *monoglycerides*). If the small intestine is taxed, it can lose control over its boundaries—allowing passage of larger, partially digested food particles that retain a signature as chicken protein, rice starch, or the oil of a certain source (proteins cause the most trouble if allowed to pass not fully digested, by the way). Since these are recognizable as "not you" by the immune system, they prompt an immune response, including inflammation (heat) that is a healthy part of that response. If small intestine leakage persists, inflammation becomes chronic and damaging. At this point two things can happen.

In the first scenario, the body, in its wisdom, acts to protect itself from inflammation by shunting the heat and offending toxins to areas within the body that are metabolically slow, commonly into fat deposits (that may grow to accommodate more toxicity) and the joints (which over time will suffer from the heat pathology they hold). In Chinese medicine, this mechanism is described in great detail as the body diverting pathology away from the core organs in a precise and predictable progression. Problems can arise and then seem to go away, but in truth they have only gone latent. Depending on the individual and the specific pathways used by their body to divert pathogenic factors to protect vital organs, a wide variety of illnesses can arise, caused by the deep, slow damage done to the area trying to safely hold this simmering, underground heat. Illnesses generally caused by this scenario include many well-known inflammation and autoimmune diseases of otherwise mysterious cause such as multiple sclerosis, lupus, rheumatoid arthritis, diabetes, fibromyalgia as well as Parkinson's and heart disease. If you are lucky and skillful enough to be able to clear out latent pathologies, your health will improve at a very deep level, but probably not without experiencing a series of healing crises that are likely to occur as latency is released and cleared. Although there is no theoretical reason this can't be done on one's own, a skilled clinician's guidance can be nearly indispensable.

The second scenario arising from leaky gut is the onset of food sensitivities or allergies. In this case, food particles not fully digested pass the intestinal filters while still carrying signatures of their identity. This alarms the immune system. Over time, the immune system (our protective *qi* known as *wei qi* in Chinese medicine) might be provoked when these foods are merely tasted, long before they reach the stomach or small intestine at all. This is an acquired allergic response. The body has been conditioned to respond to foods that have "leaked" through the small intestine walls in the past. The inflammation response has become habitual. As the condition persists and progresses, a person can become "sensitive to *everything*", all kinds of foods, perfumes, chemicals, even skin sensations and emotions. Since the nerves of the gut—the enteric or belly consciousness—are not directly available to the conscious mind, a hypersensitive individual can feel as if the body is falling apart from deep within, fearing that they have lost control of their health and their lives.

In either of these scenarios, healing is possible, but one thing is certain: continuing with the dietary status quo will prevent deep clearing from ever occurring—the body must receive a strong message of change to signal the possibility of clearing at this very deep level. A distinctive and unmistakable change of diet is essential to signal a new direction for our deep health.

» To start, eliminate sugar and gut irritants such as alcohol, gluten, non-fermented dairy, hot spices, onion and garlic (they can be used in other contexts, but not here).

» Avoid processed foods; eat real food free of pesticides if possible.

» Add foods that support integrity of the small intestine, such as fermented foods, non-glutinous grains, green vegetables of many varieties, bone broth, and the warming spices: ginger, turmeric, scallions, cinnamon, nutmeg, cumin, cardamom, fennel, star anise, and so forth.

Leaky Gut Syndrome

"Leaky gut" has an informal sound to it. In medical circles, the condition is called "increased permeability" or IP, aptly describing the situation: incompletely digested food particles pass through the permeable walls of the small intestine when they shouldn't.

In Chinese medicine, holding things in place is a function governed by the pancreas-spleen. In other words, the integrity of the body's internal boundaries rests on good digestion and metabolism. This system needs to be strong, an aspect of a hidden, internal physical fitness of the metabolism.

It is also very important that the mucosal lining of the intestines is sufficient. An extension of stomach yin, this protective-yet-permeable gut lining is supported by an artful balance of foods that soothe and those that move. A good strategy is to increase soothing soups, stews and breakfast porridge while also increasing fiber-containing foods: whole grains and vegetables, including those that contain special fiber types such as inulin (celeriac, beets, asparagus, leeks, etc.) Since increasing fiber may be irritating at first (due to deficiency of appropriate gut microbes), adjust slowly but steadily, with an achievable plan.

Causes of Leaky Gut Syndrome

Leaky gut syndrome is an increasingly common issue. Some may say it is a "fad diagnosis". Fad or not, increased porosity contributes to or causes many conditions if you know what to look for, particularly because so many people have taken a lot of antibiotics and pain medications that are damaging to the stomach and small intestine. Every dose of such medications should be followed by deliberate restoration of the gut through foods we now think of as encouraging repair of the stomach, pancreas-spleen, small intestine and the microbiota:

» Gentle, soothing foods (white rice, millet, sweet potato, chia pudding, yogurt, miso soup, etc.)

» Foods that aid descension and clear food stagnation (cooked carrot, whole grains, almonds, figs, warming spices, etc.)

» Meals that digest easily (see Clear Meals, chapter 9)

» Fermented foods (yogurt, miso soup, pickled vegetables, sauerkraut, kombucha)

» Sprouts and germinated grains (mung sprouts, microgreens, germinated rice, millet, barley, etc.)

Leaky gut can arise from various causes or their combinations. These causes include damage from diet, damage from antibiotic use, damage from pain medications or other drugs, and damage from pesticides, herbicides and preservatives. Let's approach these one at a time.

Damage from Diet

Here are the main culprits when it comes to dietary damage of the small intestine:

- » Excessive sugar

- » Allergy or sensitivity to gluten or dairy

- » Excessive cold food/drinks

- » Overeating

- » If small intestine lining is weakened or inflamed, irritants including onions and garlic

- » Poorly combined meals (often just adding dessert overly challenges digestion)

- » Erratic or rushed eating times

- » Eating while stressed or fatigued (even if accustomed to fatigue)

- » Excessive alcohol (relative to the individual, to some extent)

Damage from Antibiotics

Antibiotics can save lives, but their use causes varying degrees of damage to the stomach, pancreas-spleen, small intestine, and especially the living gut microflora. Some clinicians claim a degree of leaky gut syndrome will take place in anyone who has had even two courses of antibiotics at some point in their life. While others feel this is overestimating the damage done by antibiotics, the point is well taken. Antibiotics were developed in a time when all microbes were naively considered potential germs. Now it is known that any use of oral antibiotics—no matter how necessary—damages necessary intestinal microbes.

There are perhaps trillions of microbes living in the human intestines. Each finds its own specific area to which it is perfectly adapted (some are so well adapted to their unique habitats that they have not been grown successfully in the lab for study). It is not well understood how this microscopic ecosystem works, but it is thought that the colonization of specific areas by healthy microbes keeps dangerous ones from proliferating in the same location. Antibiotics unintentionally wipe out these well-balanced populations, leaving their terrain open for less desirable players. When healthy, not only are the good microbes tolerated, they are necessary for digesting some nutrients, manufacturing others, neutralizing bile and hormones for safe excretion, all functions required for good health.

A Word on Antibiotics

I am not opposed to the use of antibiotics. At the same time, it's easy to see that they are overprescribed, and their side effects often minimized or ignored. Add to this the present danger of supergerms that have become immune to treatment (due to overmedicating humans and farm animals) and the casual use of antibiotics becomes impossible to support responsibly.

Antibiotics need to be reserved for life-saving applications only. When not life-threatening, it's often better to treat infections or suspected infections with other methods. When antibiotics are truly needed, nurturing back the stomach, small intestine and the microbiota should accompany treatment and continue for several months after treatment concludes. Use probiotic drinks or supplements, fermented foods, simplified meals, and foods that directly benefit the small intestine.

Damage from Common Analgesics

Nonsteroidal anti-inflammatory drugs—including over-the-counter pain pills and prescription drugs labeled as NSAIDs—also damage the stomach and small intestine, setting the stage for the development of digestive problems such as leaky gut syndrome and the systemic inflammation that can follow. NSAIDs are generally considered safe, but they are not without side effects. Anyone with weak digestion, or specific problems such as colitis, inflammatory bowel disease (IBS), or Crohn's disease should be especially mindful when considering their use.

> » NSAIDs include: aspirin of all brands and types, *ibuprofen* such as Advil or Motrin, *naproxen* such as Aleve, and many other drugs, often with multiple brand names.

> » Tylenol (*acetaminophen*) is not an NSAID—it lowers fever and eases pain but

doesn't reduce inflammation. Therefore, Tylenol is not considered especially problematic for the small intestine, but it does strongly tax the liver, and
should be used with earnest restraint. (Tylenol is currently the leading cause of
acute liver failure in the United States.)

» Pain management requires artful care, balancing genuine need with protecting
the stomach, intestines, microbiota, and liver from damage.

» Although not NSAIDs, opioid pain medications, whether necessary or otherwise, are very stressful for the intestines, leading to such severe stagnation that
a new class of laxatives is being marketed specifically to opioid users.

Damage from Pesticides, Herbicides and Preservatives

There is increasing evidence (sometimes hotly contested by the manufacturers) that certain common farm chemicals linger in foods and are able to breach the membranes of the small intestine.
They are, after all, neither food nor familiar to the human gut, so we have no protections to handle them. It could be that some individuals are more susceptible to chemically induced leakage
than others. What is significant is that these chemicals—the very common herbicide *glyphosate*,
known as Roundup, is one of them—pass through the protective membranes of the small intestine wall. Further, glyphosate chemically binds with substances normally safely constrained by
the epithelial membranes of the small intestine walls, carrying them through and into the bloodstream and lymphatic system. Glyphosate and other farm chemicals often found in foods can act
as carriers across the small intestine filter, allowing dangerous substances to enter the blood in
what can be understood as a chemically induced leaky gut syndrome.

As an example, aluminum (a common element in the environment that is sometimes absorbed
into food through cooking surfaces) normally cannot cross the small intestine wall. In healthy
individuals, the small intestine is capable of perfectly preventing aluminum and similar toxins
from crossing into the blood and lymph system. However, if glyphosate and aluminum are present together, their combination cannot be held back, particularly if other stresses have weakened
the intestine wall. Aluminum (a neurotoxin if allowed into the body) has been found in the
pineal glands and brains of individuals who suffered from Alzheimer's and other diseases. Farm

chemicals such as glyphosate may be a crucial cofactor ferrying toxins such as aluminum across the small intestine membranes.

This brings up the next major point—breaches of the intestinal membranes (leaky gut) correlate strongly with breaches of another key filter system: the blood-brain barrier. While this is to be expected according to Chinese medicine theory (a failure of pancreas-spleen dominion regarding maintenance of boundaries throughout the body), continued research is needed to confirm or otherwise clarify these findings from Western medicine point of view.

Based on what we do know, individuals who are showing signs of increased gut porosity (leaky gut syndrome) or are suffering from chronic illnesses including neurological or autoimmune issues, may find it prudent—or even necessary—to avoid foods containing farm chemical residues or preservatives. Many modern crops have been genetically modified specifically to tolerate high volumes of these chemicals, so it is particularly important to select organic non-GMO foods, as much as is possible.

Because warnings about aluminum cookware were widespread, most people now avoid cooking with aluminum pots and pans. It follows that we should also avoid chemical additives that allow aluminum and other nonfood chemicals to pass through our intestinal filters in a way they otherwise wouldn't.

Recovering from Leaky Gut Syndrome

Once the gut is "leaky," healing requires a twofold approach:

> » First, avoid foods (and medications, if possible) that continue irritation of the small intestine. Irritating foods may be surprisingly individual and require sensitive detective work to identify, but some are very common offenders: sugar, dairy, gluten, garlic, onions, hot pepper, bell pepper, cold foods and drinks, alcohol, coffee and chocolate. Personal food allergens will damage the gut and should be carefully avoided. Overly processed foods are generally of poor quality with some degree of rancidity masked by preservatives and artificial flavoring; naturally these foods are difficult to digest and contribute to irritation problems and more. Sometimes simply avoiding what perpetuates digestive trouble is enough to allow digestion to heal and recover.

» Follow the small intestine eating advice outlined above to adapt your diet.

  * Include soothing foods

  * Include stomach, pancreas-spleen and small intestine foods

  * Avoid foods that stress the liver and gallbladder

  * Use the Clear Meals approach for complete digestion

  * Avoid overeating or erratically timed meals

  * Sleep enough

  * Include fermented foods

  * Include kitchen herbs and spices

  * Resolve constipation or diarrhea with grains, seeds, vegetables, legumes, kitchen herbs, cooked fruits, and so forth

Why Do I Crave Sugar?

I often hear this question in the clinic. In fact, sugar cravings are very common when pancreas-spleen function is disturbed. The progression is often like this:

» The pancreas-spleen has been taxed by too much simple sugar, too much highly refined flour, too much dairy, eating when upset, overly tired, or with erratic hours. This has caused us to gather dampness (water weight or phlegm) and fatigue in the limbs and posture—a sense that life itself is too much heavy lifting.

» Then, digestion looks for quick sugar to supply blood sugar for mental alertness and physical energy, rather than doing the more valuable work of digesting and extracting blood sugar from complex carbohydrates in well-balanced meals. Remember, the brain's energy comes nearly entirely from glucose in the blood (blood sugar in common language). Low blood sugar starves the brain (lethargy, headaches, depression), and your own brain will come up with fast ways to get you to feed it, healthy or otherwise.

What Happens When Sugar Is Added After a Meal

If digestive vitality is very strong, we can enjoy a sweet finish to a meal and digest things quite nicely. If, however, we do this too often or digestion is compromised, the synchronization of digestion is badly disturbed by sweet dessert.

Digesting complex carbohydrates is the natural way to provide blood sugar for the brain (blood sugar is the brain's sole food except during prolonged deprivation when emergency energy sources can be used). Blood sugar comes from carbohydrate digestion. If simple sugars—sweets—are combined with a full meal, digestion of the complex carbs and proteins halts as the simple sugars are used to satisfy blood sugar needs. The main meal sits in the moist and warm belly, not being digested—perfect fodder for the wrong type of intestinal microbes. In other words, our main meal ferments because our brain and muscles have had their blood sugar needs fulfilled. Fulfilled, that is, until blood sugar levels crash from the excess insulin secreted to meet all that quick sugar that has rushed into the blood. This is when most people go to sleep, sufficiently tired from their day and taxed by dinner. If you stay up, blood sugar levels can then go too low, as insulin and other hormones force sugar out of the blood and into our cells. A wave of sugar craving may arrive, or the desire for caffeine (or both as a chocolate craving, "dessert for dessert", in a real sense). All this time, dinner is fermenting rather than digesting well. The next morning you will be groggy, digestion will be a bit weaker.

Simply put, digestion will stop working on complicated foods in favor of available simple sugars, leading to cravings and the wrong microbes proliferating in the gut. The answer is to eat dessert only occasionally. Eat fruit between meals. Eat meals that you personally can digest well.

Craving sweets is natural when you are tired in a way that sleep doesn't satisfy. Blood sugar is low, a situation we call *qi deficiency*. Eating sugar—often with refined carbs, for example in pastries, cookies, or energy bars—is by far the easiest way to raise blood sugar. Unfortunately, sugar further damages pancreas-spleen energetics, leading to a feedback loop of trouble. At some point it is essential to cut this cycle with personal discipline. For most people, getting to the other side of sugar cravings takes about two weeks, during which time you eat plenty of good food but avoid any added sugar or highly refined carbs (eating gently sweet real foods like sweet potato can help during cravings). After the first week, improvement will be noticeable. By the end of the second, you will have won the battle.

What Is the Simple Take on Leaky Gut Syndrome?

Leaky gut is in many ways an illness of modern life, arising most often from a history of anti-biotics damaging the "healthy" microbes of the gut combined with high sugar consumption that subsequently feeds the "unhealthy" microbes that remain. Once the intestinal flora is out of balance, population blooms fed by easy sugars and refined carbohydrates can cause serious problems.

NSAIDs can be involved as well. In Chinese medicine terms, underlying leaky gut syndrome is a history of damage to the energetics of the stomach and pancreas-spleen; healing depends upon restoring those energetics. Feeling better can begin immediately, but problems like leaky gut syndrome can take a long while to fully heal. In my clinical experience, some relief can be expected from the first day or two, but full recovery requires 3 to 9 months of careful eating.

Many people report beginning to feel better after their first clear meal—in other words, as soon as they begin having meals that are nourishing, delicious, and within their personal capacity to digest well. With leaky gut syndrome, however, improvement gained can be lost quite easily by returning to what caused the problem. Good understanding of how these problems arise and knowing you have the tools to fix them is very helpful to sustain motivation.

ELEVEN

Helping the Small Intestine Through Serious Illness: Chronic Lyme, SIBO, and the Mysterious Condition Known as *Gu* Syndrome

Human health is very resilient, capable of thriving on widely different diets and warding off illnesses quite effectively. But when this natural resilience seems to fail, it is important to assess the role that digestive problems have played in weakening the robust health that we all want and should be able to enjoy.

Often in the clinic, we see links between undiagnosed leaky gut and chronic illnesses. When a hidden leaky gut scenario coincides with exhaustion, an individual can become dangerously vulnerable to infectious disease or autoimmune conditions. For example, a rested person may be exposed to an infection such as Lyme disease and do well with a course of appropriate antibiotic. But someone who is already exhausted, stressed, and depleted may remain ill even after many courses of the same treatment. Antibiotics work best when a person's own immunity is also engaged. If immunity is compromised through fatigue, dehydration, stress and chronic inflammation, even multiple courses of antibiotics are sometimes not successful. Complicated scenarios of co-infection and latency can result. If the small intestine and microbiota are already compromised, antibiotics will damage the microbiota further—tolerable damage if the antibiotics quickly resolve an infection, but a serious concern if they do not.

Many people suffering from conditions that don't conform to standard diagnosis often miss the digestive component that holds their illnesses in place. Patients tend to either ignore digestion because their specialists don't speak of it or reach for supplements and superfoods that may be potent but lack a well-crafted strategy. Attempts at self-medicating are common and often counterproductive, mixing treatment approaches too freely, throwing internal energetics into significant disharmony.

One way to know if small intestine issues are involved with a scenario of chronic illness is through telltale emotional signs: the small intestine emotional signs are about "not feeling like myself", feeling foggy or confused about why I am experiencing these emotions, or a sense of disconnect from experience. When illness lingers beyond conventional medical treatment, it is important to focus on restoring digestion and fundamental health before attempting again to rid the source of the illness.

> ### Small Intestine in Simplest Terms
>
> *The small intestine separates things for us that we eat or experience. It separates what we can use from what is garbage (to us). The small intestine sends along what can't be easily digested, first to be "composted" by microbes to extract more nutrients and then eventually for elimination.*
>
> *The small intestine also helps handle things within the body, protecting the heart from what is "too hot to handle": physical or emotional toxins. The small intestine's role is essential and done with thankless perfection, but for some people it becomes overwhelmed.*

What Is SIBO?

Small Intestine Bacterial Overgrowth is a condition of yeast, fungal, or bacterial colonization in the upper small intestine, an area that normally is host to only a small population of helpful microbes. Usually caused by antibiotics wiping out the natural balance of the microbiota, a steady diet too high in sugar and dairy, or damage done by unhealthy weight-loss dieting, SIBO feels like having a yeast farm in the middle of the body that fizzes when the "wrong" foods are eaten, causing bloating and distention. Symptoms can arise very quickly upon eating. Beyond the bloating from yeast or bacterial gas (like bubbles in beer), those suffering from SIBO often have nausea, diarrhea, fatigue, generalized joint pain, and can have malabsorption of nutrients from food, sometimes leading to anemia and bone loss.

SIBO can arise along with other illnesses such as diabetes or Crohn's disease, as the function of the small intestine loses integrity. It often occurs along with or underlies common problems in the lower bowel known as *Irritable Bowel Syndrome* (IBS). The medical test for SIBO is simple: a breath test checks for the presence of hydrogen gas in your breath after drinking a test fluid high in fructose (fruit sugar) and lactose (milk sugar). If digested well, very little hydrogen is in one's breath, but if yeast or bacteria digest the sugars, their byproducts include substantial hydrogen, easily detected in a lab as the patient blows into a balloon every 15 minutes for 2 hours. (Remember, most beneficial microbes are meant to live in the second and especially the third section of the small intestine; relatively few colonize the first part. SIBO is an overgrowth of opportunistic sugar-eating yeasts and bacteria in the uppermost section of the small intestine, where they shouldn't be.)

Lactose Intolerant?

Lactose intolerance can cause bloating, distention, pain, and diarrhea. It is not a dangerous condition and is generally self-diagnosable. Like all mammals, humans gradually lose the enzymes to digest milk after weaning age. Most adults do not produce sufficient lactase enzyme to digest milk sugar (lactose). Some estimates are that 75 percent of the world adult population is dairy intolerant. The ability to digest milk as an adult can be seen as a special adaptation and not the norm; this adaptation is highest among northern Europeans and their genetic relatives, but lactose intolerance occurs in this population as well.

Rather than worry about lactose intolerance or purchase specially manipulated dairy products, simply skip dairy if you don't digest it well. The dairy industry has falsely advertised milk as an essential food for building or maintaining strong bones. On the contrary, bones are nourished and protected by ample vegetables with moderate but not excessive protein. Excess protein (including that from dairy) weakens bones by leaching minerals from the bones to neutralize acids left in the blood from metabolizing protein. For most adults, it is advantageous to have little or no dairy. Those who can't have dairy can relax knowing that this is normal. Protect your bones with plenty of green vegetables daily.

Diagnosis of specifics can be important, but treatment should always include prudent dietary support. Lactose intolerance can be a cause; removing all dairy (at least for several weeks as a test) is important. Sugar feeds the yeasts and bacteria blooming where they don't belong; it is very important to deprive them of easy food by strictly eliminating sugar (including "natural" sugar like honey or maple syrup), fruit, and refined grain (especially pasta and bread). Applying the Clear Meal principles will fine-tune specific food choices (what makes a meal for you that digests well, fully and in timely fashion?). Recovery is often swift. After initial improvement, diet needs to be maintained to avoid blooms recurring (they will, if we are not vigilant!). In time, your personal clear meal repertoire can expand.

Although SIBO has complexities, remember that it is sugar that feeds these microbes that have colonized and bloomed too high up in the small intestine. Handling SIBO requires strict discipline with sugar and carbs. It is common to see people suffering with SIBO who still include sugar in their diets, despite being very strict with other foods.

What Is *Gu* Syndrome?

In classical Chinese medicine, the term *gu* is used for complex chronic illnesses originating with digestive problems, including possibilities of "bad" microbe overgrowth or parasites accompanied by some degree of emotional discord. The written Chinese character for *gu* looks like a vessel containing three worms. These can be understood as germs, microscopic parasites, visible intestinal worms, or other problems. As the condition of *gu* progresses, emotional involvement is inevitable (in ancient times, ghosts or possession were sometimes implicated as well). Today we don't blame ghosts for our problems, but patients in the clinic do give reports like this:

> *I was doing fine, and then I got sick…I took antibiotics, but it didn't help, my doctor says it's psychological, but I know something's wrong physically…my blood tests are inconclusive… maybe there's a parasite or resistant germ, we don't know…but I feel like I'm not myself, I don't recognize myself anymore….*

In modern terms, *gu* syndrome can be understood as multiple opportunistic infections afflicting a person already suffering from deep depletion and stress, with emotional distress clouding life's experience. Causes of energetic depletion can be overworking (self-motivated or otherwise), emotional stress (loss of job or a death in the family are common factors), or any of the dietary stress factors already discussed. As mentioned in the Lyme disease example, a person encountering a germ or parasite when already depleted can experience a scenario of multiple opportunistic infections ("infestation" would be closer to the original meaning) that often resists treatment.

Gu syndrome can be a useful way to look at difficult conditions like chronic Lyme disease, which can be considered a leaky gut scenario with possible complication of parasites. (Yeast, fungus, or other "bad" microbes are, in a sense, parasites, the labels are widely overlapping.) Some clinicians point out that first-world doctors dismiss the possibility of parasites too quickly, noting that parasites can easily be introduced from around the world to any modern town or city. Today's food supply is global. But even if classic parasites are not present, *gu* syndrome treatment strategies provide a powerful way to work with deeply seated digestive problems involving microbial imbalance or overgrowth.

Gu syndrome strategies usually requires a multiple-phase approach.

Latency Phase

First, assess if the patient is strong enough to fight the infections (often multiple), or if it is better to maintain latency (keep symptoms quiet) while dramatically building strength to get ready to fight the infections at a later date. If many rounds of medications and other treatments have not been successful, building strength first is necessary before proceeding. Once strong enough to begin the stage of fighting the pathogens involved (germs, microbes, parasites, etc.), proceed to the stage of *dispersing pathogenic factors*.

Disperse Pathogen Phase

Aromatic herbs are used to disperse stagnant toxins. The image in classical Chinese medicine is the idea of bringing light to hidden places in the body, places where toxins and germs have found latency. If you feel light—in both connotations of lighting up dark corners and light rather than heavy—then you can succeed in recovering from *gu* illnesses. In classical herbal medicine there are a number of key aromatic agents used that are also kitchen herbs. These are very important for the dietary approach to penetrate into the damp turbidity and promote healing:

* Mint

* Shiso (sometimes called Japanese mint)

* Chrysanthemum (can be found as chrysanthemum tea)

* Scallion

* Citrus peel

Weakening the Pathogens Phase

When the first two stages are fulfilled, the next phase can begin, classically called *killing the parasites and expelling the demons.* That is not common talk among practitioners today, but people I see with chronic Lyme or parasite-like conditions often speak in language very similar to this, apologizing first then saying, "I know this sounds weird, but it's like something has got me and I no longer have control." In any case, killing and expelling is done with stronger dietary players:

- Onion

- Raw garlic

- Clove

- Turmeric

- Betel nut (a fairly strong laxative)

- Bitters (Dietary bitters include dandelion greens, broccoli rabe, endive, chicory, and the others listed earlier. Cocktail bitters can be used and are increasingly available. Select a brand without sugar, then boil to remove the alcohol before adding drops to hot water for sipping.)

A very common mistake is to embark on this phase when not yet strong enough to enact it. Many of the parasitic agents involved in *gu* syndrome have sophisticated defense tactics that are triggered by challenge. Since they wouldn't be present if the immune system were not somewhat compromised, it's likely they will not be weakened, killed, or expelled until the person is much stronger, regardless of the food, herb or Western medicine applied.

It is essential to treat difficult cases like these in sequential order:

» First, *build strength.*

» Second, use brightly aromatic foods (or other herbs) to *open the nooks and crannies.*

» Then use stronger herbs and spices to *kill and expel* the parasites, fungi, parasites, viruses or spirochetes that may be working together in an afflicted individual.

Meanwhile, it is also necessary that the rest of the diet is very clean, avoiding sticky foods like dairy, sugar, gluten, and heavy foods that prevent the "light" from reaching into the internal corners (in other words, providing "sticky harbor" for latency). Instead of eating the sticky foods that sabotage successful treatments, tune the diet to accomplish three remaining aspects of the healing strategy: *build blood and nourish qi, invigorate energy and blood*, and *calm the spirit*. These are big subjects, so let's look at each in a little more detail.

Build Blood and Nourish *Qi*

We all have enough blood to bleed, but blood is not always ample and rich. At this stage we eat to nourish or tonify blood and the energy of life. Foods that build blood include:

» Soups made with beef or chicken with root vegetables such as carrots. Building blood with vegetarian foods is a little more difficult but definitely possible.

» Grains like rice or millet help build blood by restoring stomach and pancreas-spleen function.

» Small red beans (adzuki or red lentils) help build blood without adding to stagnation.

» Root vegetables are rich in minerals and other required nutrients (beets and sweet potatoes, but also carrots, parsnips, turnips, etc.).

» Berries (blueberries, blackberries, raspberries, goji berries).

» Green vegetables (kale, collard, broccoli, bok choy, cabbage, spinach, chard, etc.).

» Eggs also help build blood—particularly if matched with porridge or soup such as such as Egg Drop Soup (see page 93 of Book 2).

Invigorate Energy and Blood

In Chinese medicine there is an important dictum: whenever you enrich the blood (through well-pointed nourishment and improved digestion), you must also invigorate the blood, that is, get things moving. Fatigue leads to stagnation and stagnation leads to fatigue—therefore building and moving need to work together. From a dietary point of view, it's easy to understand that if you don't do this, the richer foods will feel heavy and lead to even more sluggishness in blood circulation. That helps us know what foods will be helpful at this stage—foods that clear stagnation are aromatic and uplifting. I put dishes and meals together at this stage that feature the following:

» Asparagus, celery

» Bean sprouts (gently cooked) to provide protein while clearing and lifting upward

» Spices such as rosemary, oregano, parsley, cilantro, dill, tarragon, mint, shiso, fresh ginger, turmeric, and citrus peel

» Seed spices are needed to prevent or resolve bloating and distention: fennel seed, cumin, cardamom, coriander, caraway, anise seed, dill seed, or celery seed.

» Warming may be needed to scatter cold causing stagnation. If so, include also cinnamon, nutmeg, and clove.

» Cooking with red wine invigorates blood, particularly with the warming spices mentioned.

» Garlic can provide a boost to the blood (if not already overused).

» Bitter greens are also important here: dandelion greens, radicchio, endive, chicory, escarole, broccoli rabe, bitter melon, and so forth. Bitter greens nourish but also clear heat and stimulate movement (downward). It's important when invigorating not to stimulate too much heat or upward movement. Avoiding hot spices and including bitter greens is important.

Calm the Spirit

Here the focus is not on psychological or meditation techniques for establishing calm; we are interested now in what foods help loosen the somatic foundations for mental distress and insomnia. Some hint of these problems may be familiar to most of us, but remember, if our systems are fundamentally strong, we may get very sick, but it's not *gu* syndrome. *Gu* syndrome is identified by three factors together:

> » Multiple synchronous infections by pathogen: parasite, fungus, mold, yeast, spirochete, etc.

> » A pre-existing weakness

> » An emotional or psychological component, often exacerbated by sleep disturbance

As mentioned in chapter 8, the psychological or emotional problems associated with the small intestine are closely related to the heart, but with a twist. There is a quality of being surprised at oneself: I don't understand why I'm acting and feeling this way…I don't recognize myself…I want my life back. These feelings can sometimes reach a feverish peak of emotional upset. Stress and digestion are deeply linked (see next chapter on *adrenals, stress* and *digestion*), so calming the heart is essential for genuine recovery from *gu* syndrome or any chronic condition involving digestion, leaky gut, or intestinal problem.

In Chinese herbal medicine, there are a number of substances known to both calm the heart and clear parasites. Dietary therapy, however, doesn't use such strong substances. We use foods as our tools, but the strategy is largely the same.

> » Lotus seed is traditionally used here, and it's a beautiful food (find in China-town markets).

> » If lotus seed isn't in your market or likely to be on your plate, use more common seeds such as sesame or poppy seeds. Sesame has a grounding effect and poppy seeds have a connection with heart energetics.

> » Adding ground flax seed can help clear intestines, making life harder for parasites.

> » Mushrooms are useful here, calming the spirit while strengthening the kidneys.

> » Pistachios are a calming nut with a natural heart affinity.

> » Adzuki beans also exert a calming influence on the spirit. (They are my go-to food for connecting heart and kidney—in other words, opening and awareness

link between our experience of our own lives and our inborn imperatives. Said simply, adzuki beans help link the heart with the kidneys, shining light on how your individuality fits with your family psychological inheritance.)

» Root vegetables and seaweeds anchor the emotions.

» Diuretic and bitter vegetables (snow peas and radicchio, for example) are important for draining "bitter experiences" physically away from the heart itself. Metaphor and science work together to help our hearts be free.

Although this is an abbreviated tour through a therapeutic dietary protocol for certain difficult cases, it may still seem complex. And it's true that most people do not have the multiple opportunistic infections based on compromised immunity described as *gu* syndrome. Still, it is helpful for all of us to learn that we can use foods to help heal situations that may feel impossible to overcome.

TWELVE

Tending the Pilot Light Within:
The Role of the Kidneys

Beneath the functions of all the other organs (including digestion in all its complexities) lies the cornerstone, the slow-burning candle flame known in Chinese medicine as *kidney yang qi*. Generally speaking, *kidney yang* corresponds to adrenal health in Western medicine. Like a hidden pilot flame that lights the big fires of digestion, the *kidney yang* fire sustains all our vitality, including not only our internal organs and system functions, but also our consciousness, identity, and ambitions.

From a modern biomedicine point of view, the basic functions of the kidneys are:

» To filter wastes from the blood

» To filter excess water to maintain fluid balance and help regulate blood pressure

Therefore, to help the kidneys, we should:

» Maintain healthy weight (avoid obesity)

» Maintain healthy blood pressure (hypertension eventually damages kidneys)

» Avoid smoking and alcohol excess (known to damage kidneys)

» Avoid overuse of over-the-counter and other drugs. Common drugs known to cause kidney damage—at times severely—include:

+ Nonsteroidal anti-inflammatory drugs (NSAIDs), e.g., ibuprofen, naproxen, or aspirin in higher dosage. (Tylenol, the brand for acetaminophen, is not an NSAID and is considered safe for kidney function, but is hard on the liver. Care should be taken.)

+ Antibiotics

+ Chemotherapy and HIV drugs

» Some blood pressure medications

» Illegal or recreational drugs

» Ulcer medications

» Dyes used in medical scans known as *contrast media*

» Dyes used in pills and other medications

As in modern biomedicine, classical Chinese medicine also speaks of the kidneys filtering blood for toxins and sensitively adjusting blood volume. This is the "fluid regulating" aspect of the kidneys. Beyond basic physiology, the kidneys are also related intimately with the deepest levels of constitutional health. The kidneys govern:

» Maturation and waning of fertility

» Bone integrity (including particularly the spine, hips, knees)

» Bone marrow

» Brain health

» Hormones

From very different starting places, classical and modern medicine agree: as the deep health of the kidneys declines with aging (or is well-maintained), reproductive health, bone density and robust mental function also declines (or remains well-maintained).

Defining Kidney Yin and Kidney Yang

Originally, yin referred to "dark" or "shade", as in the shaded side of a forest tree that is cool, moist, and covered with moss. The yang side of the tree faces the sun and is dry and without moss. This originated in the Naturalist school of thought in ancient China: everything large and small works according to grand principles observable in the natural world.

Applied to health many centuries later, yin is about substance, coolness, moisture, and repose. Yang refers to moving energy, brightness, warmth, and action. Kidney yin, therefore, is a collective term including the hormones of the constitutional level; kidney yang is a

> *collective term for the moving role of the kidneys (actively cleaning blood) and the invigorating role of the hormones from the adrenal glands. This is not merely poetic theory, it allows us to associate common foods with essential but hidden health functions.*

All *yin* is complemented by *yang*, as substance and energy work together to maintain the infinite complexities of life. *Kidney yin* (supporting deep constitutional health at the structure level) is complemented by *kidney yang*, represented in Western terms by the adrenal glands, small but powerful glands situated on the top of each kidney.

The Adrenal Glands Do the Following (Simply Stated)

» Produce stress hormones, essential for handling trauma (from a small cut to severe injury), including illness, infections, fear, emergencies, and happy stress such as getting married, stage fright, first day at new job, and so much more of daily living.

» Produce essential hormones that govern blood sugar and the metabolism of proteins, carbohydrates, and fats (all three *macronutrients*).

» Produce sex hormones that regulate bone mass, muscle tone, how stress is experienced, libido, and aging cycles.

» Produce hormones involved with blood pressure regulation. (But don't forget that most people with blood pressure problems have the type more associated with liver than kidney. High blood pressure caused by the liver is the type associated with emotional stress, deep frustration, or high-pressure ambition.)

» Note: most of these hormones are best understood as *kidney yin*; *kidney yang* is also known as the *moving qi of the kidney*, which includes adrenaline.

As mentioned above, Chinese medicine views the adrenal glands as something like a pilot light, a small, perfectly situated flame necessary for lighting the internal cooking fires that fuel the transformations we call *digestion*. Now it's easy to see the connections between the adrenal glands, digestion and stress. Secretions from the adrenal glands are essential for metabolizing protein, fats, and sugars. No secretions, no metabolism. Since the adrenals also make stress hormones, severe or prolonged stress directly impacts digestion. Stress taxes the adrenals so that they are not up to fulfilling their other functions. Cause and effect can sometimes be separated by time; for this reason, digestive problems caused by stress can simmer under the radar. This is a problem of digestion not being supported by the deep health of the pilot light: pancreas-spleen not receiving sufficient *kidney yang qi*.

The Fire Beneath Digestion

Digestion is energized by sufficient kidney yang, like a pilot light within a stove. It doesn't do the cooking, but the flame that does "cook" our food relies upon it deeply. We mustn't run our daily energy from our kidney flame (adrenals), but if our kidney flame is weak everything else is weak, too.

This is a critical point to understand: *beneath the organs of digestion lie the master support for all digestion and metabolism, the adrenal glands, sitting atop the kidneys.* This is a hidden pillar of good health. Since, in Chinese medicine, the kidneys are associated with a person's constitution, the adrenals are therefore part of *prenatal qi* (inborn, constitutional, inherited, genetic). The food we eat is of course *not* inborn, it is from the outside world, and therefore digesting it provides *postnatal qi*. In this way, there is an intimate relationship of *pre-* and *postnatal qi*, leading to a second hidden pillar of good health and longevity: *prenatal qi fires the digestion and assimilation of postnatal qi, while postnatal qi provides our daily energy, thus protecting prenatal qi from becoming depleted.*

Prenatal Qi and Postnatal Qi

Simply put, prenatal qi refers to your constitutional reserves, your very deep health. This is inborn.

Your postnatal qi energy is acquired through food, water, sunshine, and emotional nourishment.

Prenatal qi is needed to support the digestive organs that gather postnatal qi from food; postnatal qi in turn protects prenatal qi.

We have already learned that when digestion becomes weakened, we become vulnerable to problems like gaining weight, developing a paunch or spreading hips, pre-diabetes, leaky gut, or *gu* syndrome. Any activity or experience that repeatedly calls on stress hormones diminishes adrenal capacity to support digestion. This includes extreme stress from violence, displacement, poverty, or any fear at the survival level, including being subject to prejudice or racism. Stress hormones are also taxed when working late, relaxing late, eating and sleeping at erratic hours, and eating too much sugar, fats, and proteins (all require adrenal secretions for digestion).

Sustained stress (common in modern living) chronically taxes the adrenal glands. The masters of classical Chinese healing encourage us to treat our *kidney yin* and *kidney yang* as precious jewels. Why would we treat our precious glandular reserves with any less care than we would give to emeralds or rubies?

Use Your Own Words

Classical language is eloquent and helps us understand the lineage of this wisdom. At the same time, if you can't say something in your own way, you don't really understand it. Using your own words can be an exercise in real understanding.

I have a friend who likes the phrase "living off your glands" to mean running your daily energy from adrenaline fueled by caffeine. If he hasn't had his coffee, he can't speak to anyone or do anything. This is his version of saying that if you don't digest postnatal qi, you will be tapping prenatal qi to get through the day. In other words, food well-digested is like adding wax to the burning candle—you won't use up the wax the candle was made with. If food is absent, poor quality, or not digested well, the candle will be burning its own wax. Living off the glands is like cooking from the pilot light. It's difficult, every day is hard, and it saps our constitutional strength.

What are your ways of understanding this idea for yourself?

Kidney Yang Depletion Is Similar to Adrenal Exhaustion

In Western terms, *kidney yang depletion* is often called *adrenal exhaustion*. With this in mind, it's clear that further stimulating the adrenals is not a good idea. More coffee increases adrenal exhaustion; what is needed first and foremost is more rest and less stress. Restoring adrenals takes a bit of time—weeks or even months. It does not happen with one night of rest or a nap after work. Nor does it happen with a vacation including stressful flights and lots of activities. The way to successfully restore the *kidney yang* aspect of health is to:

» Be asleep by 10 p.m. Consistent sleeping on this schedule is far more effective for restoring deep hormone health than eight or even more hours of sleep beginning at midnight or later. Try it and you'll see.

» Avoid stimulants and excessively stimulating activity, including digital screens at night.

» Sleep in the dark.

» Finish all eating at least two hours before sleep.

The Foods for Kidney Health

If we understand that the kidneys not only filter blood but also serve as a basis for hormonal health and good digestion, we realize that we should treasure this level of deep reserve. What, then, makes a good kidney food? How do we support our kidney status with our daily eating?

Foods that help kidney function are first differentiated between the preservation of constitutional health (*yin* aspect) and the active functions (filtering action, the adrenal functions, *yang* aspect). Usually, it's best to begin with nourishing *kidney yin*, because that (including improved sleep) will automatically support *kidney yang*.

Foods that help *consolidate* the constitutional level (*kidney yin*, deep hormones, bones, etc.) include:

» Shellfish, including clams, mussels, oysters, abalone, and scallops. All life begins in the sea; it is natural that seafood nourishes our deep, constitutional health reserves. (Note: shellfish that turn red when cooked are stimulating to *kidney yang*, not constitutional essence. The shellfish that turns red are shrimp, lobster and crab. Avoid these while specifically nourishing *kidney yin*.)

» Fish can also be kidney food, resonating with the mysterious source of all life, the oceans (and the associated salty taste). White fish, however, lean more toward a liver and lung resonance and less for kidney affinity; it is as if this type of fish is in evolutionary transition toward the meat of land animals. The fish that nourish *kidney yin* are the oily types: salmon, mackerel, anchovies, sardines, and herring (forming the acronym SMASH for easy recall). Their oils nourish *yin* and provide raw materials for restoring harmony of hormone levels and glandular interactions.

Kidneys are about constitution, including reproduction (the passing along of constitutional genetics). Kidney foods therefore include foods related to reproduction.

» Eggs are the reproductive aspect of poultry; they resonate with our constitutional level when we eat them (eggs from chicken, quail, duck, goose, etc., including fish eggs, also known as caviar).

» Seeds, beans and nuts are the reproductive kernels of plants and likewise connect with *kidney yin*. It is important to note that the oils (fats) in nuts, seeds, beans, shellfish and eggs are necessary for hormone production; often I see people (mostly, but not only, women) who are suffering from deep depletion at the *kidney yin* and *yang* levels due directly to following very low-fat diets. A low-fat diet is not a well-balanced diet; include eggs, seafood, nuts, beans, seeds and good quality oils to nourish the deepest level of health.

» Sesame seeds nourish kidneys. The color associated with kidneys is black or the very dark blue-green that you would see diving into the ocean and looking up to the sky through deep water. Therefore, black sesame seeds, black beans, black soybeans, and so forth are said to have a special kidney connection. Black sesame seeds are a traditional favorite for two signs of kidney weakness: premature graying or loss of hair.

» Rich, long-cooked animal foods such as bone broth or stews support the constitutional level of health we are speaking of here. Pork, by the way, is considered a particularly kidney-supporting meat. In my practice I often recommend pork for this purpose, although I personally avoid it. Personal preferences can always be respected, work-arounds found without any stress or fuss.

Vegetarian foods that benefit kidney health are mushrooms and seaweeds (and the seeds, beans, and nuts just mentioned above).

» Mushrooms thrive in very damp, cool conditions, popping up overnight after a rain. Mushrooms help clear our internal dampness (including fungal terrain) when we include them in our diet.

» People in coastal Asia have developed an extra enzyme or two that help extract more nourishment from seaweeds. Sea vegetables (as we might more respectfully call them) nonetheless strongly support small intestine and kidney health for everyone, even for those who may not digest them as fully as a Japanese fisherman (later we'll see that the intestinal microbiota can digest foods that we don't digest directly). Sea vegetables are also important for thyroid health, protecting to some degree from radiation pollution in the food supply. Some folks who focus on disaster preparedness keep a stash of seaweed on hand to eat at the first sign of radiation danger; the idea is to fill the thyroid with healthy iodine from seaweed, so it won't absorb radioactive iodine.

» Diuretic foods (foods that promote urination) also support healthy kidney function (steady use helps protect from kidney stones). The most common diuretic foods are the bean pods: string beans, snow peas, sugar snap peas. Adzuki beans are not sold with their pod but drinking their cooking water as a broth nourishes kidney health and includes diuretic qualities (then eat the beans if digestion is strong enough—adzuki beans are an excellent kidney food). Slightly more adventurous kitchen people can make a broth or "tea" from fresh or dried corn silk, gathered from sweet corn in the summertime. Corn silk tea is an excellent diuretic, making room for healthy fluids as water retention clears. Corn silk tea is a very common Chinese kitchen remedy for edema (swelling) of the legs, arms, and face. Roasted barley tea (very common in Korea) is also an effective diuretic. Barley soup can be used if preferred; I often recommend barley soup not because it is better but because it is more familiar to most and therefore more likely to be used regularly.

Foods that support *kidney yang* (adrenal function) include:

» Shrimp, crab, and lobster—the shellfish that turn red when cooked (as mentioned above).

» Game meats such as venison. (Think of how alert and on guard deer are compared to domesticated cattle. Wild game, especially venison, has a very strong adrenal connection.)

» For vegetarian options to support *kidney yang*, add *yang qi* to seeds and nuts by dry-roasting them in a heavy skillet. *Yang qi* is added both by the heat (medium-high) and the constant movement in the pan (to prevent burning). Oven roasting is acceptable but misses the physical moving aspect. Be careful not to burn them. Add roasted nuts and seeds to dishes or snacks. (Soaking nuts and seeds overnight is always good—the "almost sprouting" that soaking provides also encourages *yang qi*, adding an ascending gallbladder energetic to the seeds to aid their digestion. Dry the soaked nuts and seeds in the oven on lowest setting, then dry-roast in a heavy pan as described.)

Diet for Adrenal Exhaustion

If adrenal exhaustion is present, all digestion will be affected, as described above. Therefore, begin by being gentle. Follow the advice for restoring stomach, pancreas-spleen, and gut integrity (congee, steamed grains, vegetables, soft foods such as zucchini or sweet potato, root vegetables, and the Clear Meal principles). Then, focus specifically on the adrenal issue with these points:

» Avoid stimulants, including coffee and chocolate (green or oolong tea are fine for most people). Wean off coffee slowly—for example, down to 1/2 or 1/4 cup daily, then eliminate completely. This will minimize headaches compared to stopping a substantial habit suddenly. (A dietary patient comes to mind who arrived with a 16-cup per day coffee habit, wondering why he felt tired, irritated, and so easily prone to anger. We started by switching 8 of his 16 cups to decaffeinated, then he gradually reduced to 1 cup in the morning. Past that he was not willing to go, but he is feeling great, and incidentally, is in a solid romantic relationship for the first time in years.) Weaning to little or no caffeine is possible and advisable to restore adrenal health.

» Avoid foods identified or suspected of causing sensitivities, inflammation, or allergy for you personally (culprits can vary). Ongoing use of foods that you react poorly to keeps your adrenals continually stimulated as part of the inflammation response.

» Stay well hydrated. Drink one or two glasses of room temperature water first thing in the morning. Continue to hydrate not only with water but with wet-cooked foods (often better for hydration than plain water).

» Sugar is a stimulant and is in direct relationship not only with insulin (a hormone of the pancreas) but also with the hormones of the adrenal glands. Eliminate sugar and processed foods (including "natural" sugars such as honey, maple syrup, agave, etc.) Rely instead on a variety of grains for well-regulated blood sugar (including at least some whole grains, sweet potato, or squash). Overcoming sugar cravings usually takes about two weeks to complete.

» Eat healthy oils and foods that contain healthy fats (including eggs, butter, olive oil, nuts, seeds, avocado, etc.) Oils are needed to make adrenal hormones. A common mistake is adopting an overly enthusiastic low-fat diet, which deprives the adrenals of the raw materials needed for hormone production, interfering with stress-management, and often making the transition into menopause more difficult. Dietary cholesterol, by the way, is important for hormone production. Reducing cholesterol for those living a stressful life or through stressful times can lead to deficiency of necessary stress hormones, a common instance of well-meaning dietary discipline leading to psychological and physical problems. Welcome eggs, olive oil, nuts, seeds, avocado, coconut and butter, in amounts appropriate for you as an individual.

» Eat animal foods for their strong *yang qi* (as always, good health must respect personal ethical or religious rules, adjust accordingly). Vegetarians can use nuts, seeds, and beans with warming spices.

» Include the *kidney yin* and *kidney yang* foods listed above, and the general eating advice to restore digestion: soothing foods, simplified clear meals, fermented foods, and all that we have discussed previously.

» Warming spices support *yang qi*: cinnamon, fresh ginger, turmeric, nutmeg, clove, rosemary, oregano, dill, cumin, star anise, mustard seed. Warming spices are not hot spices, please note. Hot spices (chili pepper, onion, garlic) will dry up fluids if used in excess. Remember that *kidney yang* depends upon sufficient *kidney yin* including good hydration; dryness will damage this balance.

» Accept that stress management is an important aspect of personal health, that few of us handle stress well enough, and adopt a personal stress-reduction plan, including time in nature, meditation, yoga, qigong, etc. Self-expression is crucial for everyone. "Being heard" by family, friends, colleagues, and acquaintances is a matter of good health. Actively appreciating or participating in the arts is also essential to a healthy life.

» Organize your sleeping and eating schedule to be more aligned with the natural cycle of daylight. Many people live with continual jet-lag, waking and sleeping out of synch with their location (even without having traveled). This taxes the pineal gland, increasingly seen as the master gland of the body since it regulates the timing of so many essential functions. Often, chaotic eating and sleeping schedules sabotage efforts at health and healing, including for people who are trying really hard to get better in other ways. Work gently to restore a more natural sleep rhythm, being careful not to add more stress to an already stressed system as you try to sleep earlier. We are not nocturnal animals. Adjusting to a daylight waking cycle may take some time, but it is so important that it should be a part of everyone's health practice. (Reasonable exceptions are expected, of course, for a night out, or adjusting to travel.)

Resolving adrenal exhaustion usually takes quite a while, mainly because most people refuse to make sufficient lifestyle changes such as taking a break from stress, realigning sleeping-eating cycles, or adjusting diet. With commitment and clarity of what to do, improvement can be noticeable within days, substantial within two weeks, and virtually complete in three months. Because adrenal exhaustion or *kidney yang depletion* so commonly underlies or is entangled with serious chronic illness, the value of addressing it successfully can't be overstated.

It's important here to acknowledge that adrenal-related problems can be complex. Sleep disturbance, for example, can be a *symptom* of adrenal exhaustion (and digestive stress), not just a cause. Don't give up if it feels difficult at first. Small progress with either sleep habits or with diet will help you be able to make changes with the other, establishing a gradual loop of improvement.

THIRTEEN

Inhaling the Breath of Heaven: The Role of the Lungs in Digestion

Food is about spirit. A good meal is an offering. To eat it is to receive the offering. Good digestion requires an enthusiasm for life—if we are dispirited, frustrated or pessimistic, we already have poor digestion. If digestion is weak, it means we can't handle what the world has to offer. We can't sort what is good for us from what we don't need or can't assimilate. This is the wisdom our bellies must have and that we must protect. Digestion is a living metaphor as much as a physical function.

Intrinsic in this equation is breath, metaphorically provided by the sky, or if you prefer, the atmosphere. Life requires substance (*matter*) and something indescribable, something like a *spark*. As in familiar Creation stories, heaven provides the air and spark needed to make substance come to life. This meeting of spark, breath, and earth is an ongoing miracle, in one way of speaking. Breath maintains the spark that ignites food from the earth to sustain life. In practical terms, this means breath descends to meet digesting food in the belly and to fan the spark of life held as our pilot light, that is, our *kidney yang*.

> » Air enters from above (*Da Qi, heavenly qi*).

> » *Da Qi* descends as breath (sufficiently deep breathing).

> » Breath (originally from heaven) stokes our pilot light, firing the transformations we call digestion, assimilation, and metabolism.

Two aspects commonly go wrong here:

> » Breath is shallow, lacking *descension*.

> » The kidneys fail to grasp the descending *lung qi*.

This poetic classical terminology is worth including, not only for its intriguing charm but because it leads us to something very important: good living depends upon not only sufficient breathing and not only deep-enough breathing, but upon a subtle exchange when breath is deep. There needs to be a slight pause when breath is full and deep. When we exhale, something essential remains below, nourishing the spark of *kidney yang* in the belly (some people experience this in the lower back). When this is working well it is hardly noticeable, there is nothing artificial in it. When it's not working well, some deliberate effort can help recover a beneficial way of breathing we may have lost years ago.

That's is only part of it, however. The process just described is like a bellows. Breath comes down to fan the fire needed to transform our food, fanning the deeply hidden flame of *kidney yang*, which in turn maintains *stomach fire* itself. That's the first image.

The second image is of a third flame (or spark), this one in the heart. The essence of food is allowed to pass through the "smart barrier" of the intestinal walls to enter the blood. In the classical view of Chinese medicine, this is still not enough. The food's essence must rise to the chest, where it combines with fresh breath in the lungs—*Da Qi*. Only then is it ready to be circulated by the heart to all parts of the body. This process, called the *completion of postnatal qi*, occurs in the chest: breath mixes with blood that has been enriched with nutrients assimilated through the intestine walls, before being pumped through the body for the cellular combustion we call *metabolism*.

Heart as the Heart of Compassion?

The heart can't digest food or mix blood with oxygen. But what the heart can do has been associated with love and compassion for ages. The heart waits for food to be assimilated, then moves this nutrient-rich blood to the lungs to be mixed with breath, and then, when the blood is filled with the gifts of earth and heaven, the heart adds some kind of spark before spreading this blood to every cell in the body, without judgment or favorites.

To meditate on the heart, first locate the warm spark of the heart that brings spirit to the blood it circulates. Then try to locate the spreading quality, following blood to every cell. Then start again, following nutrients entering the blood in the belly, receiving breath in the lungs, entering the heart, experiencing some kind of firing, then spreading to all cells. This simple contemplation practice unites all uses of the word heart.

What is digested in the belly separates into two—the "impure" material continues to descend toward the large intestine and eventual elimination, while the "pure essence" of the food ascends to the chest where the lungs and heart preside over the mixing in of the last essential ingredient, the spark of life itself, breath (oxygen, if you prefer) and something entirely insubstantial from the heart. When this goes well, we are supported by the fruits of the earth and the breath of heaven, to use classical language; we are living on these gifts. We are energized and inspired. If it goes poorly, we lack enthusiasm and are tired even after eating good food.

Although poetic, this terminology points to two very precise things:

» An ascending energy is required after digestion has extracted nutrients.

» Mixing these nutrients with fresh breath is needed to complete their transformation into energy and body substance.

Supporting Metabolism

Metabolism requires oxygen. It is a process like micro-combustion, a little furnace working in each of our cells. Modern science provides incredible detail on the complexities of the metabolic process, but too much detail can be disempowering, leading many to think only drugs and supplements with scientific names can meet the challenge of supporting our internal functions. This is unfortunate. We need something practical we can do at home to support and restore healthy metabolism. Here is what we can do:

» Eat good foods that fit within what you can personally digest well.

» Don't overeat—fill your stomach only two-thirds of the way, leaving the top third open for breath. Every culture has their way of saying this. Of course, the stomach stretches rather than fills like an empty bucket, and breath doesn't actually go into the stomach (much), but this simple image was the way two Tibetan lamas explained it to me many years ago during a transmission of their dietary healing traditions. It's simple, and I like to pass it on as it was given to me. If you fill your stomach all the way, breathing will be difficult and assimilation of the gifts of good food will not be efficiently completed.

» Include directional foods to support the natural process of uplifting and transporting food's pure essence to the chest and from there to all the corners of the body. *Descending* foods are important for digestion and elimination (grains, root vegetables, beans, nuts, seeds) but here our interest is in *uplifting* and *spreading out* (leafy greens, sprouts, germinated grains, fermented foods, and spices).

» Avoid fads that promise to increase metabolism. Use of stimulating substances or foods is likely to raise heat, with negative consequences over time. The best strategy is to avoid foods that cause dampness and hurt digestion, add exercise and breathing practices to your lifestyle, and follow dietary advice like that presented here.

The role of breath in digestion may seem very subtle or even mysterious, but a well-trained practitioner of Chinese medicine can discern the status of lung and breath functions quite clearly by reading a person's pulses (pulse reading at three positions on each wrist is a highly evolved classical art providing enormous diagnostic insight when practiced well). Even then, however, too often acupuncturists or herbalists apply treatments without teaching what the individual can do for him or herself. All treatments can be made much more powerful by us doing our own part, cultivating breath as part of good diet.

Even for those who have no interest in Chinese medicine dietary wisdom, connecting breath to the kidneys, belly, and chest can strongly help basic health and the efficacy of any medical treatment. This connection is frequently the principal thing that is missing—what I like to call a person's "health headline". A newspaper has a lot of stories in it, just as an individual's health has many (infinite!) details, each significant and complex. But what's the headline? What is the main story that we need to know first? Often, it's that we are not combining breath with digestion, not using the bellows to fan the fire below and bring the spark of life to what we've digested as it begins its circulation in our blood.

Breath Must *Descend* and *Diffuse*

The two aspects of healthy breathing are that:

» *Lung qi descends.* This requires the relaxing of the diaphragm (the great dividing muscle between the chest and the belly), so that energy of the breath can descend into the physical area of the belly. This is deep breathing, or to be more precise, successful descension of *lung qi*.

» *Lung qi diffuses* (spreads to all areas) with an enthusiastic openness. Breathing opens all the way to your skin, to your pores. With a little quiet focus, you can experience this for yourself.

A Simple Qigong Breathing Practice

Sit comfortably, spine and neck relaxed but aligned.

Exhale, then pause for a few moments with your breathing open but empty. This is called an "open empty hold" (be careful that your breathing pipes are open).

When you are ready, when you feel a gentle but clear urge to breathe, give in to the urge, allowing breath to rush in. Pay attention to the quality of that breath. Is it deeper, more open? This simple exercise focuses on the exhalation and a pause while exhaled, but it is the following inhalation that we are cultivating.

Try again. This time, as you pause, relax all your breathing muscles. Then give in to the breathing urge. Notice how natural your breathing can be, open and deep, without discipline or effort. Continue breathing in this open manner for a series of breaths, perhaps 9 or 10, with no effort or judgment. Each breath will be different.

Practice this several times daily. Remember, each person is unique, and you must not challenge yourself too much with a long open empty hold. Practice comfortably, starting where you are today. Benefits will come naturally.

What Foods Can Help Lungs Descend and Diffuse?

Foods that support the lungs and their energetics are:

» Apples, pears, and Asian pears are the fruits that connect directly with the lungs. They help the lungs stay moist and flexible (while the two distinct types of fiber in their peels and their flesh aid with descension).

» Almonds are the main nut for the lungs. They also help moisten and clear the intestines (opening the way for breath to descend deeply). All nuts are descending and benefit the intestines with their oils and fiber, helping the lungs by clearing stagnation of the lower belly, thus opening the way for deeper breathing. Walnuts, for example, would be a good choice to supplement the use of almonds.

» Classically, anything from pine trees is used to benefit the lungs—think of inhaling the scent of a pine forest and how pine has the capacity to clear phlegm. For this association (and through generations of observation) pine nuts are also considered a very important food for the lungs.

» Fresh ginger root warms digestion and helps clear the lungs. Fresh ginger is very important and can be used daily. Other spices have clearing influence on the lungs, each in slightly different ways, such as mint, cilantro, dill, rosemary, and many others.

» Daikon is a root vegetable that helps *lung qi* descend. Its gentle radish sharpness helps the lungs clear.

» Citrus peel relaxes the diaphragm. The diaphragm easily gets tight, constricting the ability of the lungs to descend and bring breath to the belly and lower back. Citrus peel is wonderful for opening breathing and assisting digestion. Traditionally, dried ripe tangerine or mandarin

Drying Citrus Peels

Purchase organic tangerine or mandarin oranges. Wash the outside of the fruit. Save the peels after eating the flesh sections. When possible, dry the peels in warm sunshine, spreading them out on a clean surface, allowing air to circulate around each peel portion. You may also dry the pieces in an oven set to lowest temperature for 1-2 hours, with the door ajar to avoid trapping moisture or overheating the peels. Dry until the peels are very light and stiff to the touch. A food dehydrator also works perfectly for this process, if you have one.

Leave the peels uncovered for a day or two to ensure dryness before storing in an airtight container. (If not fully dry, the peels will rot; if well-dried they will keep on hand nearly indefinitely, ready for use in cooking or mixed into a kitchen remedy tea.)

To use, break off a small bit the size of one or two square inches. The flavor is very pleasing but strong—a little goes a long way. The peel can be removed after flavoring a dish, or left in if slivered very finely.

peels are used, but any citrus will contribute. Pesticides need to be considered here. Because farmers don't expect the peel to be consumed and pesticides are designed to stick past rains if possible, pesticide residues can be hard to clean off. Best is to use the peel of organic citrus. When you find a batch of organic citrus, the peels can easily be harvested and dried for storage. Use the peel and the white pith, but for these purposes do not use the fruit inside.

» The lungs like a well-regulated moistness. This supports their elasticity. Millet is an excellent grain for moistening the lungs and treating a dry, hacking cough (use steamed millet or millet porridge, recipes for both in Book 2). If too wet, lungs get depressed with mucus or phlegm (use warming, clearing, aromatic spices to help clear dampness from the lungs, including fresh ginger, scallions, citrus peel, cumin, cardamom, grain of paradise, fennel seed, caraway seed, mustard seed, cinnamon, oregano and rosemary). Dry-toasting grains before cooking adds *yang qi*, which helps digestion in its aspect of uplifting, helping the connection from the middle region (stomach, pancreas-spleen and digestion) with the upper region (lungs, heart and circulation). Many of the ideas presented earlier for assisting pancreas-spleen and gallbladder are applicable here (use of sprouts, dry-toasting grains, fermented foods, digestive spices, and clear meals). Dry-toasting spices amplifies their benefit for clearing lungs and is common in Indian and Mexican cuisine, among others.

Spices or Herbs?

In the kitchen, leafy and bulb aromatics are usually called herbs while the term spice is used for seed aromatics and a few others. Rosemary, oregano, basil—these are kitchen herbs, as are ginger, garlic and onions. Cumin, mustard seed, cinnamon, clove, nutmeg, cardamom—these are spices.

I use those distinctions in a kitchen context, but when the discussion gets more therapeutic and more influenced by herbal medicine, I tend to refer to all kitchen herbs and spices as spices, so there is no confusion with medicinal herbs that are not used in cuisine. Fortunately, there are many medicinal herbs that are kitchen herbs or spices, providing some especially potent tools for the cook. Look to the context to understand why some kitchen herbs may be called spices at times.

What Hurts the Lungs That Should Be Avoided?

Learning what suppresses functions is often more important than adding the specific foods that benefit them. Avoiding distress while adding support is a complete approach. Food and drink that insult the lungs must be considered.

> » Drinking cold liquids is a common dietary habit that prevents the lungs from working well. Cold drinks pass closely between the lungs on their way to the stomach. The body warms the cold drinks; the cold drinks cool the body. The lungs don't like this and try to push out the cold, sometimes with small, interrupted coughs. This coughing is directly stimulated by the cold and is the lungs' attempt to rebel. We should get the message, but often we don't, and if continued, this *cold insult* begins to constrict the ability of the lungs to descend and diffuse (to breathe deeply and openly).

> » As mentioned above, overeating "leaves no room for breath". We may experience it simply as having a belly too full to allow free breathing.

> » Food stagnation—perhaps from habitually combining foods poorly—slows down digestion. The stomach slows, delaying passing the chyme to the small intestine, which also works slowly, delaying assimilation of the nutrients and *qi* of the meal. Only after the essential nutrients (called *pure essence*) are extracted can they rise up to the chest to meet the heart and lungs to complete *postnatal qi* production. Feeling sluggish after lunch is a clue that the uplifting aspect isn't working well. In simple terms, this means that poor digestion delays the role of the lungs, often so much that the lungs don't contribute much at all.

> » Chronic constipation is common. This is also stagnation, further down the alimentary canal. With chronic constipation, the descension of food and *qi* slows dramatically. This leads to a reversal of healthy directionality. There is nowhere for digesting food to go—appetite wanes, lethargy sets in, and the natural fire of the stomach can get pushed up causing acid reflux or GERD (as well as chronic inflammatory conditions). Clearing constipation will automatically benefit lung and stomach function (since these two organs are only healthy if descending directionality is working well).

How We Chew and How We Breathe Can Improve Digestion of Any Diet

The importance of breathing into our food is similar to the importance of chewing well. The very same diet will work dramatically better if well-chewed, for a number of reasons:

» Chewing breaks food open so digestion juices can enter more thoroughly.

» Chewing stimulates salivation.

» Chewing stimulates the stomach meridian's energetics through jaw movement. (The key points on the stomach meridian of acupuncture lie on the jaw.)

Breathing into the belly and opening the chest for the completion of *postnatal qi* will also dramatically change the quality of digestion and nourishment—even without changing your diet in any way. Of course, we have discussed how certain foods help the lungs more than others, and food choices are important to clear problems, like the sense of constriction across the mid-torso that can block descension of breath into the belly. Therapeutic use of the foods mentioned above can be crucially important, but all the same, it's nice to know we have the tools we need with us wherever we go, all we have to do is cultivate our use of them. Chew well, breathe deeply.

Lungs and Digestion: An Easy Summary

Eat well, don't fill your stomach to the brim, breathe into your belly to fire the pilot light, and open the chest to complete the conversion of food into *postnatal qi*. Let the heart circulate what is now not only nutrition, but nourishment. Substance, fire, breath.

FOURTEEN

Exploring the Mysterious Ileum

Now that we understand how the kidneys, adrenals, and lungs relate to healthy digestion, we can return our focus to the lowest third of the small intestine, the *ileum*.

First, let's briefly review the first and second sections of the small intestine.

The *duodenum,* or first of three divisions of the small intestine, can be thought of as an extension of the stomach, because it is well-lined to withstand the intensely acidic chyme as it is released from the stomach. (In fact, the pyloric release sphincter that separates the stomach from the duodenum is triggered to open when the stomach's contents reach a sufficient level of acidity, along with other signals.) This specialized lining (a practical extension of *stomach yin*) also allows the duodenum to digest proteins and accept the caustic bile from the liver and gallbladder that gradually neutralizes acids (along with pancreatic secretions). A few types of specially evolved microbes live in the duodenum, but nothing like the hordes living further along. If microbes proliferate here, bloating, distention and other problems occur. If allowed to progress, this is called small intestine bacterial overgrowth, or SIBO. It's very important to clear SIBO in any cases of autoimmune disorders.

You may remember that foods for assisting the healthy function of the upper aspect of the small intestine include:

> » Foods that stimulate secretion of bile (dill, rosemary, asparagus, artichoke, celery, grapefruit, lemon, carrot, dandelion greens and radish)

> » Soothing foods that support *stomach yin* (white rice, zucchini, congee, oats, chia, etc.)

> » Root vegetables: carrots are perhaps easiest, cooked if digestion shows any weakness, but also parsnips, beets (beetroot), rutabaga, daikon, turnip.

> » If stomach acid is determined to be low, naturally brewed apple cider vinegar can be helpful (1 teaspoon to 1 tablespoon, neat, or in a glass of water, before protein meals).

The *jejunum* is the second section of the small intestine and can be thought of as the location of the digestive functions governed by pancreas-spleen, the place where most carbohydrates (grains and sugars) and fats (lipids or oils) are digested and passed through the epithelial membrane into the blood and lymphatic system. The food slurry known as chyme is no longer acidic; carb digestion must take place in an alkaline environment (pancreatic enzymes require it). Large numbers of microbes have evolved to colonize the various nooks and crannies of the jejunum, some so mysteriously perfected for their unusual habitat that they have yet to be successfully grown and studied in laboratories. As digested particles pass through the membranes of the jejunum into the bloodstream and lymphatic system, most of the water keeping the chyme wet is absorbed as well, rehydrating the body while beginning to solidify what is left to form the stool for eventual elimination.

As a reminder, some of the foods that support the functions associated with this portion of the small intestine include:

> » Soothing foods support all of digestion, especially the jejunum (sweet potato, butternut squash, zucchini, white rice, congee, millet, oats, barley, chia, okra, seaweed, etc.)

> » Sprouts (bean sprouts, sprouts from alfalfa, broccoli, kale, daikon, etc., and sprouted or germinated grains)

> » Flax seeds, chia seeds, pumpkin seeds

> » Root vegetables and whole grains

> » Green vegetables

> » Fruits (Fruits are best as snacks between meals and in their whole form. Be careful of too much sugar—especially from fruit juices—and too much cold, particularly from tropical fruits eaten in cooler than tropical climates.)

Now we're caught up. You may recall that we had paused at this point on our digestive tour to consider the adrenals, kidneys and lungs and their direct role in digestion. I chose this spot to discuss the kidney and lung aspects of digestion not because those organs are physically located there (although the kidneys are indeed close by) but because the gastrointestinal tract itself is divided into upper and lower aspects. This division can be identified by the location of the *suspenso-*

ry muscle, which is found, with some individual variation, in the upper section of the jejunum. In an emergency, whatever is still above the suspensory muscle can be hurled upward, but whatever passes below that muscle needs to be handled downward through the system. Details are endless, but now we have an overview of what happens above the suspensory muscle. This leads us to the very special (but often ignored) lower small intestine.

The Ileum Handles Foods That We Can't Digest Easily, and That's Good News

The last section of the small intestine, the ileum, handles materials that have resisted digestion so far. While the jejunum is well-stocked with helpful bacteria (in a healthy person keeping "bad players" in check), the ileum is absolutely teeming with them, nearly a thousand types, more than a trillion microbes all told. Here, bacteria and other microbiotic citizens ferment fibrous food residues that have not yielded to stomach acids or enzymatic secretions. Before you jump to the idea that it may be best to simply avoid foods that foster fermentation via this microbial army, consider that the micronutrient B_{12} is absorbed through special receptors in the ileum, not higher up in the digestive canal where most dietary nutrients are assimilated. Vitamin B_{12}—essential in extremely small amounts for healthy nerve structure—has an intimate relationship with fermentation. And indeed, although most people harvest B_{12} from animal foods in their diet, some vegans who rely heavily on fermented products (yogurt, kimchi, miso, pickles, tempeh, sauerkraut) show sufficient B_{12} levels and admirable longevity. The evidence seems to say that enough B_{12} is created through fermentation in the ileum of some vegans *if* their diet and ileum are well-tuned to the task (it is vastly easier to absorb that vitamin from some animal food, however, such as eggs, dairy, seafood, or meats).

Until recently the lower small intestine was largely ignored unless localized problems arose. Dietary focus was on nutrient-rich foods and little attention paid to, as one medical school professor put it to a physician friend of mine, "useless roughage that doesn't give us any nutrition anyway." But if you think, as I do, that nature's design is elegant and flawless, it doesn't ring true that half the length of the small intestine—3.5 meters or 11 feet of it—is useless or vestigial. The ileum houses an absolute army of microbial players, and if it isn't well understood or supported, an insurrection is not only possible but likely. And that's exactly what a lot of people say when they arrive for their first consultation, "What in the world is happening to me inside my belly?"

Looking More Closely at the Role of the Ileum

The ileum absorbs fat-soluble vitamins (including, but not only B12) and acts like a recycle-and-re-use center, absorbing bile salts that were secreted into the upper small intestine, closer to the stomach. These bile salts, wrapped in molecules of fat, are eventually sent back to the liver for refreshing and reuse. Incidentally, common salt—sodium chloride—is also absorbed through the ileum walls into the blood stream, presumably to prevent sodium levels from falling too low, an adaptation for life preservation. The design of the ileum is telling us to avoid extremely low-fat or low-salt diets—our systems take pains to ensure enough of both.

As important as these functions are, it's hard not to wonder why they require half the length of the entire small intestine, when proteins, carbohydrates, fats and water have been nearly entirely processed and assimilated by the upper ten feet or so of small intestine (the duodenum and jejunum). Why is so much precious belly real estate devoted to functions that almost no one ever thinks about?

The answer lies in the complexity of the microbiota colonizing this area of the intestine. In a way, this is where the immune system meets the outside world, gets to know what's out there in order to stay at peace with it all. This has three main aspects:

» Sensing and responding to the microbes of the world

» Learning to tolerate healthy resident microbes

» "Good" microbes acting through fermentation on rough foods low in nutrient density as a symbiotic and essential aspect of overall nutrition

Let's look at each aspect a bit more fully.

Sensing and Responding

The density of microbial colonization of the ileum is matched by unique "sense and exchange" structures in our immune system. Our immune cells, in all their complexity, reach into the ileum through delicate fingerlike structures and return to the lymph and blood areas outside the ileum walls with information needed for managing the microbiotic population.

Where you live, who your parents are, the details of your birth, whether you have a dog or play outdoors sufficiently, what foods you were raised on—all these factors and more contribute to your unique internal microbiota. Researchers are discovering more and more ways in which your unique microbiotic army has profound influences on your personal health. For example, micro-immunologists now feel that a person's microbiota can predict if they will struggle with obesity or be constitutionally thin, tend to depression, asthma, or allergies, and more. Much of this is said to be predictable within the first few months of birth. Babies begin gathering their personal microbial community during the birthing process and soon after. (Natural birth and breast feeding confer multiple health benefits, including significant advantages from a microbiome point of view.)

The ileum is the location of the highest concentration of microbiota (it is all acquired, by the way—we are sterile until birth), and the location of our immune system's most intimate interaction with it. Huge immune resources gather here. Usually, however, the ileum is ignored unless balance fails. Problems of the ileum can underlie lymphoma, Crohn's disease, and IBS (irritable bowel syndrome).

The Spiritual Dimension of the Small Intestine

While certainly not the most poetic of internal organs—rarely appearing in song lyrics, for example—the small intestine has a central energetic role. Two basic functions of the small intestine verify the classical teaching that the small intestine tunes our awareness as social beings:

> » *The small intestine sorts and separates what is useful from what isn't.*
> » *The small intestine hosts a huge collective of microbes that is constantly changing, allowing the immune system to train in tolerating the useful while firmly destroying the dangerous.*

Our small intestines help us sort out our place in a very complex world. What can we tolerate, what can we "stomach"? What, in a word, do we welcome? At the same time, what do we reject as unacceptable, which we must either avoid or defeat? Or, what would we like to reject but can't avoid, experiences that wound us but that we have to live with, like microbes in our gut that hurt us but that we can't fully get rid of? Rejecting without having the power to be clear of something requires repression in our psychology, and this causes inflammation in the physical body. Taken together it is a situation of simmering fire, a combination of internal inflammation with an inseparable emotional component.

Digestion should be strong; internal housecleaning should be kept up to date. Then the small intestine can function physically and spiritually to help us feel at home in the world. The small intestine provides feedback; we respond to its signals even if we are not consciously aware of them. The more clearly we can sort the positive from the negative, the less stress we have living in the world (and the better we can come to relax in a world that is not "all good"). We can digest our experiences, being nourished by what benefits us, transforming what we can transform, and letting what is none of our business pass right through us.

Learning to Tolerate Resident Microbes
(and the False Dream of Living Germ-Free)

Why are so many microbes present in our bodies? With the development of the germ theory of disease and modern antibiotics, a presumption developed that we could aspire to the eradication of germs (all microbes), at least in our homes, in our food, on our teeth, on our hands, and if possible, in our bodies. This was the dream of health through antiseptics, peaking in the 1960s, but still exerting strong influence today.

Classical thinking and the ongoing discoveries of modern medicine strongly refute this germ-free fantasy.

Although antiseptics are important in some circumstances—hospital operating rooms, for one example—the overuse of antibiotics has quickly spawned new generations of "supergerms" (quickly indeed—within fifty years of the invention of antibiotics, after millions of years of human evolution). Today's germs may be killed, but tomorrow's are expected to be more lethal and increasingly immune to antibiotics. Even without exposure to supergerms, antibiotics upset the microbiotic balance in our intestines, allowing pernicious microbes to flourish.

The widespread use of antibiotics means that we are often "trading" an acute infection for damage that can lead to a chronic condition (clearing an infection but damaging the microbiota). To avoid this damage, we must be willing to make a major shift in paradigm: we must wean ourselves from dreaming of killing germs, and focus instead on supporting the integrity of our immune systems, with special attention paid to the role the small intestine plays in managing a complex microbiota. We are a collective, including a trillion or more helpful microorganisms.

Their healthy balance is crucial for our own.

Antibiotics may control germs implicated in acute infection, but chronic illnesses are very often based on damage to digestion. Even if disease-causing germs are detected, true recovery depends on restoring proper digestive function, including a healthy microbiota.

The Richness of the Microbiota of the Ileum

Why is the ileum so packed with microbes? The more we learn, the more intriguing this question becomes. As an example, let's look again at vitamin B_{12}. It turns out the receptors responsible for absorbing this micronutrient don't appear until the very end of the ileum. What's all this length for? No one knows definitively, but think of it this way: through agriculture and the gradual development of modern living, we as humans have arranged to have readily available foods rich in macro and micronutrients—proteins, carbs, fats, vitamins and minerals. We have bred fat farm animals, oceans of dairy, plump modern grains, vegetables with less and less bitterness, and of course we have made a world full of refined foods. Nearly all this food is digested and absorbed in the duodenum and jejunum, the upper half or so of the small intestine. But in early times, living in the wild, we had to gather roots, seeds, tubers, leaves, all kinds of things that are barely food. We would have been chewing for a long time, with the occasional find of berries, sweet fruits, or an animal "volunteer". Such a diet would have been very high in the fibrous foods that are not digested well by the duodenum (focus on proteins) or jejunum (focus on carbs, sugars, fats). This fibrous diet requires fermentation by a microbiotic army, and the soldiers of this army would have been consumed with the "dirt" on the food itself. The ileum would have been essential for survival, and the microbes needed to help it work would have arrived with the very foods that required them (much as the microbes that ferment sauerkraut are present on the outer leaves of cabbage).

To summarize, the modern diet has marginalized the ileum (half the length of the small intestine!) in two distinct ways:

> » First, successful farming has selected for readily available nutrient-rich foods that would have been unimaginable to a hunter gatherer. These rich, modern foods—even if labeled "natural"—are mostly digested in the duodenum

(meats) and the jejunum (carbs, sweets), requiring less involvement of the fermentation army for the relatively woody, nutrient poor foods that sustained prehistoric humans (*history*, after all, began precisely with the end of hunting-gathering and the advent of farming, only about ten-thousand years ago).

» Second, foods that *do* connect with the ileum have been actively eliminated, in the gradual adoption of refined foods available with the progression of human affluence (whole grains, legumes, and root vegetables being gradually replaced by noodles, white rice, white breads, sugar, meat, and dairy).

Since the relatively unsophisticated early version of germ theory arose and the overuse of antibiotics began, many people have suffered extensive damage to the essential microbiota of the jejunum, ileum and large intestine, leading to problems ranging from discomfort after eating high-fiber foods (beans, for example) to serious autoimmune conditions.

A Note on the Low-Carb Diet

What then, about the "Paleo" or low-carb diets, that seek to return to the robust digestive health of prehistoric humans? Diet trends often respond to imbalances of the times, and may offer welcome corrections. But from the point of view of the small intestine—the heart of the gut—it is easy to see that a diet that increases animal food intake is in large part putting even more reliance on the stomach and duodenum (while raising internal fire in response to all that meat). The Paleo diet urges avoidance of overly plump carbohydrates, in other words tries to protect the jejunum (and pancreas-spleen). By increasing "low-carb" foods like ground coconut flour there is some degree of increased use of the ileum. The intense reliance on meat, however, is a red flag for the duodenum (already working hard in the standard first-world diet) and importantly is unsustainable economically and environmentally.

A simpler and more balanced approach is safer and more effective for our health: gradually restore good digestive function in each of the three areas of the small intestine. This means:

» Balancing meat or other protein (and the digestive acids known as *stomach fire*) with protective secretions (part of *stomach yin*) in the stomach and the duodenum

» Balancing grains and naturally sweet foods with foods that aid their digestion: sprouts, fermented foods, bitter greens, seeds, root vegetables, wide-leaf vegetables, upward-growing vegetables, spices, and foods with soluble fiber (often contained within these foods)

» Including foods that specifically require participation of the ileum

Along with these simple guidelines to support the small intestine, other beneficial dietary advice and intention can be meaningfully added as fine tuning. Whatever point of view makes most sense to you, keep in mind that all foods must be digested and assimilated through the various sections of the small intestine—the health of all three parts of the small intestine is crucial.

Foods That Benefit the Ileum

What foods, then, are good for the ileum? Foods that are high in fiber, clearly. But there's a catch: if our lower intestine is weak, meaning our microbiota is out of whack, we won't be able to ferment these foods well (we won't be ready to welcome them). Without the right population of beneficial microbes, eating high-fiber foods will cause distention, pain, flatulence and other discomforts. Many people experience this if they shift suddenly to a vegetarian diet high in fiber (a vegetarian diet low in fiber is not a good idea at all—for example, lots of pasta, white rice, baked goods, sweetened foods). The key is to gradually increase fiber according to what we can digest successfully. If fiber increases gradually, the integrity of the ileum will increase as well.

Follow the basic advice for stomach, pancreas-spleen and upper intestine: avoid readily available sugar and processed foods, avoid pesticide residues, avoid antibiotics if possible, add fermented foods, rotate grains, include directional foods (especially root vegetables for descension), include spices that aid digestion (many are listed above). Probiotics can also be helpful, more on that in the next chapter.

In a real sense, the role of the stomach plays out in the duodenum (digesting and assimilating proteins, for example) and the digestive role of the pancreas-spleen occurs in the jejunum (including separating pure and turbid, light and heavy, and digesting, transporting and assimilating carbs and fats). The areas of the small intestine must be differentiated as they fulfill distinct functions. This is an interpretation of the organ functions in classical Chinese medicine theory so that foods traditionally connected with the stomach and pancreas-spleen can be effectively used to benefit the different small intestine functions. (Practitioners know that the small intestine meridian used in acupuncture has its most important functions in the aspect of protecting the heart. In earlier times, the level of small intestine distress commonly seen today would only have been caused by parasites, not by the combination of antibiotics, other drugs, and high amounts of sugar seen so often today.)

What Does "Weak Digestion" Mean?

Having a weak digestion can mean that the secretions that are needed from the stomach, liver, pancreas, adrenals, and so forth are deficient in amount or poorly synchronized in timing. "Timing" here includes the idea that the qi could be weak in those organs—in other words, the functional energy to work effectively is deficient, even if the secretions are sufficient.

In the context of the lower small intestine, weakness means:

> » *Too many "bad" microbes and not enough "good" ones*
> » *Insufficient mucosal lining (often a result of microbial disarray)*
> » *Thin or damaged intestinal lining (also a result of microbiota problems)*

Dietary weakness can lead to chronic constipation or diarrhea, leaky gut syndrome, auto-immune problems, allergy, obesity, or depression. Because high-fiber foods can't be digested well under these conditions, they are avoided, creating a cycle of increasing problems.

To break this cycle, gradually and steadily introduce more fiber, for example lentils, carrots, sweet potatoes with their skins, whole grains, apples, pears, almonds, walnuts, and so forth. Start with very small portions of these with your regular foods, gradually cutting back on processed foods as you are better able to digest whole foods.

Not surprisingly, then, much of the digestive work classically assigned to the large intestine actually begins in the ileum. Foods traditionally identified as supporting large intestine health actively support health of the mysterious lower half of the small intestine, the ileum. These foods include:

> » Root vegetables. Here it is not only the sweet root vegetables that aid digestion
>   and descension such as carrots, parsnips, rutabaga, and the "honorary root veg-
>   etables" such as sweet potatoes, and butternut squash (although do eat them

all more often!).

» Daikon radish, or the sharper tasting small, red radishes

» If you want a delicious root vegetable that more closely resembles the diet of early humans, try burdock root. It is wonderful, with a gently earthy flavor and a hint of the fibrous chewiness that would have been such a big part of gatherer existence. Burdock is available in Asian shops and good organic markets, or as a forage find in much of North America and Europe. Burdock is very long and slender; it is the deepest-growing land food in the human diet.

Cooking Burdock Root

Select firm roots. Wash them well—they are often rather dirty with soil. Peeling is optional (the skin is perfectly good to eat, but I recommend peeling when new to burdock). Slice diagonally to preferred thickness. Simmer just covered in water with two splashes of tamari and a single splash of mirin for 15 minutes, or until tender but still firm. Finish with a few drops toasted sesame oil.

Burdock can also be roasted in the oven: wash, cut into sections, brush with oil, roast at 400°F for 15-25 minutes (depending on size), finish with a pinch of sea salt and sprinkle of sesame seeds.

Burdock "kinpira" is a common home dish in Japan. Cut washed burdock into 2-inch sections, then cut each section lengthwise into quarters (like carrot sticks). Sauté in oil such as grapeseed for 5 minutes, then add tamari and sake (or dry white wine) and simmer wet for another 5 minutes. Serve with rice, vegetables and fish.

Burdock is also commonly pickled.

» Cassava (aka manioc or yuca) is another root vegetable (a tuber, technically) that connects with the ileum. Cassava is a staple for millions in South America (where it is native) and in southern Asia and Africa. Cassava is beginning to enjoy fad food status because it is gluten-free and has a low glycemic index despite being high in calories. In other words, it provides slow and steady energy while actively regulating blood sugar levels. It is increasingly recommended for diabetics and as a wheat substitute for those with celiac disease. Cassava is high in the type of fiber that cannot be digested either in the duodenum or the jejunum. These carbohydrates are digested by the microbiota of the ileum. Nutrients are then available, but equally important is how this type of fiber helps restore a healthy population balance in the microbiotic army. As the microbiota improves, healing of the intestinal wall and mucosal lining follows.

* Tapioca is a familiar (if old-fashioned sounding) refined starch made from cassava. It has some of cassava's benefits for blood sugar balance but does not benefit the microbiota of the ileum since it has had the beneficial fibers removed.

* Cassava must never be eaten raw since it contains cyanide compounds similar to those found in apricot pits or apple seeds. Traditionally, cassava is soaked in water, the water is discarded, then the starch is then well-cooked, a process that safely neutralizes its toxicity.

» Whole grains also are a good source of the *insoluble* fiber that feeds the micro-farm of the ileum. (Refined grains are not helpful here; they are high in carbs and the *soluble* fiber associated with jejunum digestion.) Oats, brown rice, whole barley, rye, whole wheat, and millet are beneficial to both the jejunum and ileum. Avoid wheat, barley, and rye if you react poorly to gluten or need to avoid its stickiness. If you can eat wheat, I recommend using historically early wheats (emmer, einkorn, spelt, kamut), particularly in preparations of bulgur (often durum wheat, a hybrid of emmer). These early wheats and styles of preparation are the best way to gain the benefits of wheat (warming, strengthening, feeding the ileum microbiota) without the problems that wheat can bring (dryness, stickiness). Oats and barley deserve special mention since they are gelatinous (soothing to upper digestion) and also contain insoluble fiber (beneficial to lower digestion).

» All vegetables include complex fiber profiles. Tubers can be particularly beneficial, along with sweet potato varieties, yams, and plantain. Edible gourds are excellent (bitter melon is especially descending and high in insoluble fiber). Parsnips, rutabaga, beets, turnip, parsley root—in the market, take a favorable look at the root vegetables that most people walk past or don't recognize (these are old-fashioned foods, good for digestion).

» Beans are high in insoluble fiber, making them difficult to digest without a well-functioning microbiotic army in the belly. Digestive spices (cumin, oregano, etc.) strongly aid digestion, but problems with beans can be seen as a warning message and not simply a reason to celebrate that we have other foods on offer in modern supermarkets. Select heirloom beans, then soak them overnight, discarding the soaking water to cook with fresh. Cook with spices but avoid salting until beans are soft. As mentioned above, if lower digestion is weak, adding earthy foods suddenly can cause discomfort. Gently challenge the microbiotic army that is in disarray (or mutiny!) by increasing dietary fiber gradually. Harmony will arrive as the members of the microbiotic orchestra multiply and learn to work well together. Begin with small beans such as lentils. Although they are much easier to digest (and tend not to cause distention), lentils are rich in both soluble and insoluble fiber.

» Many fruits and nuts have complex fiber profiles (fruit juices do not). My first choices to benefit the lower digestion are apples, pears, and almonds. These have long been associated with the large intestine in the dietary branch of Chinese medicine; they are very well applied to the ileum as well.

» Seeds moisten the intestines and promote peristalsis (helping food move downward through digestion). Ground flax seeds—mentioned as good for the jejunum—also contain insoluble fiber and are helpful for the ileum. In addition, small seeds *included* within certain fruits are specifically beneficial to the ileum and in turn the large intestine, including figs and eggplant (eat the entire food except the stem).

» In contrast to the large intestine that has a *holding* nature, the ileum is still very much a part of the very long, slender small intestine. With its many twists and turns, the small intestine favors foods that encourage descending movement. (The overall movement of the small intestine as part of the digestive canal is down and out.) Energetically (and ultimately anatomically) all aspects of the small intestine benefit from foods that encourage peristalsis, including bitter greens (broccoli rabe, chicory, endive, dandelion greens, etc.), bitter melon, root vegetables, seeds, nuts, foods high in fiber such as fruits and whole grains. Many common problems are set on a healing course by reestablishing descension of the entire digestive channel.

How Fast Is Your Gut?

Some people are considered to be "slow transporters" while others are said to be quick. Too quick can be a problem—meaning that lunch passes the stomach and intestines and appears in the stool in less than six hours; foods will not have time to be digested and assimilated (let alone fermented in the ileum). The transit time for food to complete digestion and for waste to be eliminated varies with individuals but should be at least 8 hours and not more than 48. A good goal is between 24 and 36 hours.

The simple test to discover if you are a slow or fast transporter is to swallow some kernels of sweet corn without proper chewing—these will turn up in the stool, offering information on your intestinal speed. Too long offers more time for assimilation but can be associated with stagnation, weight gain, and lower belly maladies; too short is often a sign of heat trapped in the intestines (inflammation is eventually damaging). As with so much else, regulating toward a healthy middle is key. Add more fiber foods to increase the movement of peristalsis, or add more white rice and gently sweet foods if you are currently a "quick transporter". It's necessary to have an individual strategy for how much fiber and descending foods to add to your diet and at what pace.

If all goes well, balanced healthful eating will be so successful that we won't need to know anything about stomach descension, pancreas-spleen ascension, bitter foods to stimulate bile production, *stomach yin* protection for the duodenum, seeds to soothe and promote peristalsis in the jejunum, fermentable fiber for the ileum, or any of the rest. If, however, balance gets upset (from processed foods, emotional eating late at night, overexposure to medications or pesticides, etc.), having this knowledge can save the farm. It can even be the difference between medical treatment succeeding or failing, whether modern, classical, or other. When digestion is working for us, everything can go well.

It can feel complicated, so let's simplify.

A Summary in Simple Terms

The small intestine must separate a meal into *what to absorb* and *what to pass down* for further processing or elimination. Although occasionally moving too fast (due to problems of heat over-stimulating movement, or cold not allowing digestion to "uphold"), modern foods often move too slowly through the intestines. Adding foods that aid descension is therefore very helpful for most people.

We can't expect dogmatic diets to be well balanced or healthful in the long term. These include weight loss diets, low-carb diets, no-carb diets, no-fat diets, no-white-food diets, etc. What is best is to know the specifics of your own health, understand the roles of different foods (at least in a general way) and eat a basic diet of wholesome foods, attentively cooked.

Try to avoid foods or "stuff to eat" that cause snack damage, food stagnation, or otherwise disturb efficient digestion.

If problems arise (and some problems always arise through a life), adjust diet first. If medicines are needed, make good use of them, but after a course of medications spend a month or so focused on restoring good digestion.

Include foods that are good for each area of the small intestine—in other words, eat proteins, carbohydrates, oils, and what used to be called "roughage" (now given nominally scientific names of soluble and insoluble dietary fiber). Simply put, include enough vegetables, whole fruits, grains, root vegetables, seeds and nuts to provide a spectrum of fibers.

To improve weak digestion, consider separating protein and carbohydrate meals, allowing the sophisticated sequence of secretions governed by the stomach, pancreas, spleen, gallbladder, adrenal glands, and upper small intestine to have the best shot at fully and efficiently performing their roles.

As mentioned above, general advice for small intestine restoration is to eat:

» Gentle, soothing foods, starting with true appetizers such as soups

» Foods that aid descension (and clear food stagnation)

» Meals that digest clearly

» Fermented foods

Eating specific foods to nurture the three main divisions of the small intestine can be helpful for all, and for some people, it is absolutely essential. Stay at it for a while; rebuilding digestion can be slow. It is common that well-designed meals feel great right away, even from the first, but true healing takes several months to stabilize. And of course, returning to the diet and lifestyle that caused earlier problems is pretty much guaranteed to cause them again.

Don't forget to breathe after eating. Don't eat so much that there's no room left for breath.

Above all, remember that food is a gift from the outside world that we use to support our inner world; no food would be possible—not even junk food—if not for successful pairing of the energies of the sun (above) and the earth (below). Whether we eat consciously or stuff our faces in front of a television, with each bite we are playing our part, transforming the gifts of the world into our human experience, for our allotted time.

On this spiritual note, it's time to consider the role of the large intestine.

FIFTEEN

Nurturing the Large Intestine

We don't spend a lot of time thinking about functions of the large intestine. When we do, we're usually thinking about elimination—something's wrong or something hurts. But far from merely handling elimination of solid wastes, the large intestine carries out important functions in the digestive process.

Once all three sections of the small intestine have done their work, the large intestine receives and gathers what remains unabsorbed. Simply put, food which cannot be transformed and digested in the small intestine is known by the (overly narrow) term *fiber*. Added to this fiber is a bunch of body refuse such as retired blood cells, deactivated hormones, and a legion of deserters from the microbiotic army. And while the long, winding small intestine hosts and manages many millions of microscopic friends, there are more than a trillion microbes in residence in the large intestine. In a classic case of symbiosis, this internal factory releases otherwise locked nutrients for us while we provide a continuous diet to support this inner microbial farm. It's a system that has deeply surprised modern biology in its complexity, strangeness, and importance.

Only after the microbial farmers of the large intestine have done their work is the stool ready to exit. And we all know that good elimination is one of the keys to health and happiness (along with sleep, nourishment, and emotional connection). But there is more to it. While the large intestine is doing its work, it functions as a temporary *holding* organ, and any internal toxins can cause damage as they await elimination. This becomes a very important issue for anyone exposed to environmental toxins including farmers, construction or industrial workers, artists who handle oil paints, solvents, and other toxic substances, or those who live within polluted areas. It also is a concern for people who conduct practices such as liver cleanses and fasts. If there is slow peristalsis or chronic constipation, internal toxicity can build up, harming the complex lining of the large intestine and colon. In Chinese medicine, the key question is, "Are the portals of elimination open, or is there a slowdown of urination or defecation?" Constipation needs honest and serious attention.

The focus here is on the lower portals of elimination, but systemic stagnation can also impact the

upper portals (the sinuses, ears, eyes, throat, and breathing). Health requires well-regulated openness, and congestion of the upper portals can indicate problems of digestion and elimination.
More on the relationship between respiration and the large intestine in a moment.

What Foods Will Help the Large Intestine?

We know by now that the answer must be specific to the individual and their complete current
condition, but here are some general guidelines.

Descending Foods

» Unlike the small intestine (which moves food and roughage fairly steadily
downward), the large intestine has the capacity to hold its contents, subtly
shifting forward and back. If overall movement is stalled, however, stagnation
and constipation result. Here, food energetics are far more important than
looking foremost at nutritional components. To help descension and clear the
bowels, use a variety of foods including root vegetables, seeds, bitter greens,
whole grains (if digestion is strong enough), and beans (if tolerated).

» All whole grains provide bulk and fiber, but choosing gluten-free may be important. Choose long-grain brown rice and millet, as well as the important
pseudo-grains buckwheat, amaranth, teff, and quinoa. Although barley and
rye contain some gluten, they are strongly beneficial to the lower intestines and
are often much better tolerated than wheat. Oats are even more beneficial here,
and strictly gluten-free oats are available.

» Rotating grains is also important. Rotating staple foods helps avoid problems
from overuse of any particular grain (and naturally reduces gluten, a good idea
even for those who tolerate it well).

» Beans also provide good fiber and bulk, but differentiations are important; if
large beans cause stagnation, gas, or distention, use small beans like adzuki,
mung, or lentils. If digestion is strong enough, use black beans for the lower
belly, or white beans to honor the traditional association of large intestine with
the color white.

Bitter Greens

» Bitter greens are cooling and descending, particularly useful if inflammation is present.

» *Heat* in the intestines often manifests as urgent diarrhea with a strong smell. This can be chronic (as in IBS or Crohn's) or short-lived (as in bacterial dysentery such as what travelers sometimes catch in Mexico or India).

» By the way, *cold* lodged in the intestines can also cause diarrhea, but of the runny, less smelly type; here warming spices are used while bitter greens and raw food avoided (because bitter and raw would add descension, unwanted at this time). Warming spices include ginger, turmeric, cinnamon, cumin, cardamom, and so forth, but it is important to avoid the hot spices even with cold-type diarrhea, such as hot peppers, garlic or onion. Hot spices stimulate movement. Perhaps a bit more detail is needed. Sometimes the therapeutic strategy needed when dysentery or diarrhea occur is to purge more, until whatever is offending the bowels is fully cleared out. At that point, the strategy becomes to stabilize, restrain and astringe. Restraining at the wrong time (at the onset of diarrhea) may prolong the malady, but after that, unchecked diarrhea is dangerous and should be treated. Use white rice to stabilize the intestines, congee to rehydrate, pickled sour things to astringe, fermented sour foods to repopulate good microbes—in other words, foods that soothe digestion and uplift energetics, as listed earlier. Acute diarrhea can often be temporarily controlled with sugar (use a single packet of table sugar—one teaspoon—directly onto the tongue). Sugar has a binding effect in the intestines, one of the reasons modern culture has such a high instance of digestive stagnation. Use the sugar treatment only on rare occasion.

» Most people eat few if any bitter greens (it's great when patients report that they love bitter greens, and very rare among those with elimination complaints). Bitter greens provide fiber but work mainly through taste energetics. In other words, even if we were to chew bitter greens but spit them out without swallowing, the bitter taste would stimulate a cooling and descending effect within us. Of course, it's even better to learn to cook them well and enjoy them in well-designed meals.

Figs and Prunes

» These fruits strongly aid peristalsis and elimination. Prunes are most famous, with such a strong reputation that many people snicker when prunes are mentioned or are afraid that eating a few will confine them close to home (both reactions unnecessary). Prunes have many uses. As a pit fruit, they aid digestion of meats because they bring strong *yang qi* to digestion (*yang* because they are the culmination of their tree's efforts). Their *yang qi* adds energy to descension and peristalsis as well.

» Modern biomedicine suspects several different chemicals in prunes as the active ingredient that aids elimination, but even without definitive understanding of how they work, prunes are widely recommended by Western doctors, especially to the elderly who may have slower digestion.

» In contrast to the single large seed in prunes, figs have hundreds of little seeds inside. Figs resonate even more directly with the large intestine. Snacking on figs and almonds (a large intestine resonating nut) is a strong dietary laxative (if microbial overgrowth is suspected, however, fruit is best avoided, but not before all the sugar and hidden sugar is honestly removed from the diet). A clinic anecdote: a mother brought her baby, in diapers, reporting her baby had gone nearly a week without bowel movement. As the cute baby and I were getting to know each other, eye contact and giggling, I brought half a fig from the kitchen. The baby sucked on the fig, loved the sweet taste and quickly filled his diaper—to his mother's delight. Crisis averted. Small children often respond to the energetics of foods in a very clear way.

Why Dried Fruits?

Figs are available fresh for a short season, as are prunes (called Italian plums when fresh). Both fruits spoil easily when fresh, leading to the charmingly antiquated jazz musician's term for a person sadly past their relevance: moldy fig. Once dried, figs, prunes (and apricots) store well. For best dried fruits, select those not treated with sulfur dioxide used to artificially preserve bright colors.

Drying under the hot sun adds yang qi to the fruit, tempering their naturally cooling nature. Commercial dehydration doesn't offer the influence of the Mediterranean sun but still adds warmth to the fruit.

Snacking on dried fruit can be good (mix with almonds, coconut flakes and pumpkin seeds for homemade trail mix), but even better is cooking dried fruits with wine and cinnamon (see recipe on page 163 in Book 2).

Drinking Water and Elimination

There is an important and direct relationship between consuming water and ease of elimination. On a very simple level, dehydration leads to hard stools that are difficult to pass. In the clinic, I hear many people with chronic health issues say they "don't like water" or that they get tired of drinking water.

Imagine a room filled with people suffering from serious chronic illnesses. After thanking them for their generosity and openness, ask them about their hydration habits. Most will begin by saying something like "I hydrate well," or "It's very important," or "I'm always drinking something!" But if you ask how many of them drink water, their answers often begin to sound like negotiations. "Well, I can't get water down unless it's cold and has something in it, like lemon, is that okay?" "For me, I have iced tea, all day!" "In the morning I have to have my coffee, first thing…that's a liquid!" "I have diet soda, no sugar, that's fine!" "Is seltzer water okay?" "If I drink too much, I get no sleep, I can't have any water past the afternoon or I'm up too many times in the night." I've learned in my work that most people with chronic health concerns also have issues with drinking water. If that sounds like you, it's important to become reacquainted with the pleasure of drinking plain water and have plenty of it.

Morning water is the simplest health practice. It relates to health as having good tires relates to safe driving. First thing after waking and perhaps using the bathroom, have a full glass (or two) of plain, unflavored, room-temperature water. In winter, warming water to body temperature is even better. This is before any food or other drink. The purpose is for this water to pass directly through the stomach and irrigate the intestines. (If water is flavored it indicates nutrition to the body and this process will slow.)

Chinese medicine and modern medicine agree that one basic role of the intestines is to absorb water through the membrane walls. In this way the intestines regulate hydration in the body and tune the formation of the stool. Problems here can be significant for overall health. The best time to regulate this system is first thing in the morning, before food turns on the digestive sequences. Plain room-temperature water does wonders, reaching quickly to the large intestine which, ideally, will empty before the day's eating begins. Be honest with yourself: do you drink water, or start negotiations with yourself? Do you "dislike water" and substitute flavored drinks? Do you want to argue about the hydrating qualities of beverages like coffee, tea, soda, protein shakes, and so forth? This is all negotiating, like looking at your car's tires and saying that they're still okay because there's plenty of good rubber on the sides, if not on the treads. We must be honest. The body likes water best, plain water at room or body temperature, not too hot and certainly not cold. The best water to drink is spring water or filtered water. Special options such as waters with managed pH can be useful for specific reasons, but nearly everyone will benefit from any clean water, room temperature or slightly warmer, first thing in the morning.

Hydrating Foods

Morning water functions to stimulate clearing and elimination. For *banking* hydration, moist foods are equally important. While drinking water passes through us relatively quickly, wet-cooked foods release hydration gradually, carrying water (and oils) to the intestines and therefore the entire body (use porridges, congee, soups, stews, steamed grains). Dietary medicine generally prefers eating wet-cooked foods over drinking plain water to support good hydration. True, we don't add flavor to morning water so that it is not slowed in digestion to be treated as food. But later, starting with breakfast, we need wet-cooked food precisely because it does move slowly through us, allowing hydration to be absorbed amply and steadily.

Dehydration can result from other causes too, even while drinking lots of water. There can be problems of fluid transport (use more directional vegetables, cooling spices such as parsley or thyme, and add sprouts or germinated grains to the diet). Many people include too many drying foods or hot spices in their diet, heating and drying the stomach and intestines (the central hub of fluid distribution). Garlic, hot peppers, coffee, and other irritants are very stimulating. They seem to boost vitality and immunity at first (if we are sufficiently hydrated at the time), but used long-term these energetically hot foods are drying. Over time, they deplete hydration and therefore stress our immune system rather than support it.

If the stomach and intestines become relatively dry, heat conditions develop and spread. Dryness and excess heat throughout digestion are the root cause of much of the increase in inflammation or heat conditions we see today, including acid reflux, acne, rashes, dry lips, dry skin, premature wrinkling, high blood pressure, joint stiffness, arthritis, autoimmune diseases, neurological conditions, and more.

Solving systemic dryness through skillful daily inclusion of hydrating foods and elimination of drying foods (and drinks) will certainly slow the progression of some very difficult conditions, allowing treatments to be more effective. On the other hand, continuation of drying/heating diets will impede disease management by your chosen medical treatments.

Constipation Among the Elderly

Elderly people often suffer from constipation or general elimination slowdown. The causes can be:

» *Dehydration (dry-type constipation), which requires not only more water but more oils. Nuts are excellent, providing healthy oils and fiber along with a clearly descending energy. Nuts also provide high-quality protein and micronutrients. Always check nuts for freshness, rancidity should be carefully avoided (see sidebar on nuts and rancidity on page 62). Soaking nuts in water for several hours or overnight, and then drying them in the oven on lowest possible setting makes them even more delicious and much easier to digest (90 minutes in the lowest oven setting should do it).*

» *Side effects of medications*

» *Insufficient bulk in the diet (Elderly people should have gentler foods, but these foods often lack robust fiber. Further, as appetite declines, smaller meals simply don't exert enough gravity to aid descension well enough.)*

» *The directionality of the large intestine needs to be forward (also called descending). In Chinese medicine it is understood that this directional energy is provided by the lungs. Healthy, strong lungs are energized in two ways: spreading out (diffusing or effusing, what can be called "open breathing") and descending (what can be called "deep breathing"). The open breathing/effusing aspect is crucial for good immune response during cold and flu season (sufficient immune response) and hay-fever season (not too much immune response). But it's the deep breathing/descending aspect of strong lung qi that provides the downward power for peristalsis and elimination. If lungs weaken, it becomes more difficult to eliminate. Diet needs to adjust:*

* *Add more cooked root vegetables, nuts, seeds, and legumes with digestive seed spices (cumin, cardamom, coriander seed, etc.).*

* *Foods that are drying can become problematic (toast, for example). Have toast only occasionally, in rotation with grain porridges (cream of wheat, cream of buckwheat, congee, millet porridge, etc.).*

* *Almonds deserve special mention, and now we can understand why: As we learned in chapter 13, almonds are "lung nuts", that is, they have a special resonance or affinity with the lungs (so do pine nuts, incidentally). All nuts provide a descending influence because they contain fiber and oils to move and moisten the intestines, and because by their nature they grow on trees and fall when ripe. Different nuts connect with different organs, however, and almonds have a strong connection with the lungs. The lungs and large intestine are paired organs, working closely together.*

* *Walnuts are another very useful nut for constipation in the elderly.*

What About the Opposite of Constipation?

Chronic or temporary loose stool is an important sign that the vitality of digestion is weak. In traditional language, it is likely to be a weakness of the *pancreas-spleen yang qi*, responsible for the ascending aspect (seen earlier in the discussion as providing the energy to transport nutrients upward from the basically descending alimentary canal). The pancreas-spleen also is responsible for *holding materials within their boundaries*, such as blood in the blood vessels, or in this case, the stool holding together. Internal cold makes it difficult for the pancreas-spleen functions to successfully transform and uplift. While it is true that most people would benefit by eating more vegetables of all types in part because more vegetables help to clear internal heat (inflammation) from excess meat, sugar, hot spices and coffee, the opposite imbalances can also occur. Vegetables, fruits, salads, sprouts and raw juices are very cooling, sometimes too much so over time. One sign that digestion is becoming too cool is chronic loose stool, fairly common among vegans and those following a raw food diet. A quick case story:

> A dietary client reported that she could no longer eat raw salads without running to relieve diarrhea. She was an ethical vegan and had no intention of adding meat to her diet, so the warming needed to be done through cooked foods and warming spices (ginger, turmeric, cinnamon, mustard seed, nutmeg, clove, oregano, rosemary, cumin, etc.). Warming spices help resolve the underlying cold scenario. Grains are also important to support pancreas-spleen; use white rice to bind the intestines (use brown rice for constipation). Presoaking grains simplifies their digestion, and pan-toasting dry grains (before cooking) specifically aids with the *upholding* that was lacking. We often use grains for *grounding*, but dry-roasting the grains brings out their ability to help pancreas-spleen *yang qi* ascend. After all, that's how grains grow, vibrantly reaching upward to gather sunshine (*reaching to heaven*, using classical language). For the client mentioned here, resolution of the problem was nearly immediate when she adopted an all-cooked (still vegan) diet with frequent use of the warming spices mentioned above and occasional dry-roasting of rice, millet, and other grains.

The above anecdote may be more about inconvenience than illness, but elimination issues are important signs of the status of digestion. Chronic diarrhea shortly after eating becomes dangerous, as digestion doesn't have time to transform and absorb nutrients. This can allow deficiencies to develop, including anemia (remember, strong *stomach fire* is required to digest and assimilate not only protein, but dietary iron). Another way to look at this, recalling the terminology we first discussed in chapter 3, is that the person in this case was clearing far more than building, so much so that she was becoming sick from her diet. Animal food is not required, but a good balance of building and clearing is.

Crohn's Disease and IBS

Although the resolution of the case above was not complicated, it gives us a framework for working with people presenting with more difficult conditions, including irritable bowel syndrome and Crohn's disease. These are usually hot conditions (inflammation) that also involve weakness of pancreas-spleen. It's important to trace the etiology of the condition for each individual. The causes can be:

» Primarily genetic

» Related to exposure to environmental toxins

» Resulting from damage from antibiotics or other medications

» Arising from a parasitic infection

» Due to poor diet

» Connected to psychological stress (or even a single intensely stressful experience)

» A combination of these factors

Resolution of these more serious conditions requires a strategy based on improving fundamental digestion while also addressing symptoms and the specific details of inflammation (trapped heat or *simmering fire*), all in context of the individual's uniqueness.

Because internal cold and inflammation can be influencing each other within a single person's digestion, we may have to warm digestion while also clearing heat.

To warm digestion:

» Use fresh ginger, turmeric, cumin, cinnamon, nutmeg, and other warming spices to warm digestion.

» Eat all food cooked.

» Include soothing "small intestine foods": sweet potato, steamed white rice, roasted-then-steamed millet, protein in soups (for easy digestion), porridges, congee, and so forth (foods for easy digestion have been discussed in earlier chapters).

To clear heat (inflammation):

» Include bitter greens (dandelion greens, bitter melon, broccoli rabe, chicory, endive, radicchio, artichoke, and more).

» Make use of diuretic foods (snow peas, green beans, barley, seaweeds, grapes, berries, asparagus, artichoke, celery, leafy greens, bean sprouts, and more).

» Warming spices (not hot) also help clear heat. Spices move fluids to the exterior, relaxing capillaries to allow blood flow toward the skin, as well as opening the sense portals of the head (ears, nose, sinuses, eyes, throat). This helps vent heat. Fluids must be sufficient. With these spices, both aspects of the strategy can be fulfilled: warming digestion and venting excess internal heat. Warming spices include rosemary, oregano, cinnamon, cumin, cardamom, ginger, turmeric, fennel seed, etc. Horseradish and wasabi are potent root herbs that can be used in moderation to stimulate appetite, clear stagnation, and open the sense orifices. Even cooling spices (mint, parsley, thyme) move fluids and open the exterior. Mint tea, for example, can be steaming hot but still help vent heat, useful in a summer heatwave but also for internal heat conditions.

Meanwhile, it is essential to avoid foods that exacerbate the condition. These often surprise the individual. Some detective work is needed for each person, but for any digestive tract heat condition, the usual suspects that require removal from the diet are:

» Gluten, dairy, sugar

» Hot peppers

» Garlic and onions (scallions and chives are usually okay, leeks and shallots sometimes okay)

» Nightshades: tomato, peppers/capsicum, eggplant, white potato. Nightshades are complex; they can be initially cooling but their subtle toxicity builds heat in the blood level. Avoiding nightshades for inflammatory illnesses—especially achy joints—is now common practice.

» Coffee

» Chocolate

» Alcohol

» Too much meat (increases *stomach fire*)

» Fried foods

» Poorly combined meals

When someone arrives suffering miserably with gut inflammation issues, the conversation often goes like this:

> *Me: There are certain foods that commonly exacerbate digestive problems of this type.*

> *Digestive Sufferer: Okay.*

Then I start going down the list.

> *Me: Hot peppers, coffee, garlic.*

> *DS: Okay.*

> *Me: Gluten.*

> *DS: I don't eat any of that…I used to, a lot! But I cut it out long ago, I learned the hard way I couldn't handle those….*

> *Me: Alcohol, nightshades, too much meat, or overeating difficult combinations…*

> *DS: I don't drink, I heard about tomatoes and bell peppers…I don't eat any of that stuff, none.*

> *Me: …chocolate…*

> *DS: WHAT! I read it was good for you, I have some dark chocolate every night, you're not going to take that away from me?!*

> *Me: Well, it's up to you, but if you'd like to feel better, we need to try a couple weeks without any.*

This is very common in the clinical setting, one or two things on the "usual suspect" list continue to sabotage a person's efforts to get well, sometimes chocolate, or coffee, or habitual use of the wrong spices. Once the usual suspect list is clear, we look for individual allergens or sensitivities, often surprising to someone new to food energetics (for example, many don't know that chicken is a very warming food, good for some people but for others easily exacerbating heat conditions.) It's essential to have this information and look clearly at your eating habits and how they are holding you back from better health. Some dietary effects are common to most people, others are unique. Once diet is no longer actively causing problems, further work to improve health can truly begin. If your diet continues to exacerbate inflammation (or other problems), any attempts at improvement will be slowed or even negated, whether your treatment choice is diet, acupuncture, herbal medicine, or prescription pharmaceuticals.

Can't I Just Have Ice to Cool Down?

Health management can be complex. You can't just add ice or ice cream to cool inflammation or internal heat.

From the modern medicine lens: inflammation is cellular and chemical; cold drinks or foods do nothing to reach that level.

From the Chinese medicine lens: functions slow down when cold is consumed, the body naturally tries to generate more heat. Having cold food and iced drinks can complicate or amplify heat conditions even though they are cold.

The ways to clear heat are:

» *Abstain from consuming what causes excess heat.*
» *Drain heat through bitter and diuretic foods listed above, along with sufficient water to provide exit.*
» *Vent heat by opening pores using spices.*

Adding "Good Bugs" to the Intestines

What about the healthy intestinal bacteria? Do the so-called "good bugs" help with the issues we've mentioned, and if so, how do we nurture healthy microbes?

Study of the microbiota is so new that most doctors have yet to work the ideas into their practice. Dietary studies from as recently as twenty years ago are being revisited with an eye for the role of intestinal bacteria that had been completely overlooked when the studies were done. Without doubt, the expanding market of probiotic supplements will continue to grow, but the question remains: Can we get living bacteria to the lower gut without them being killed by gastric acids as they pass through the stomach? Or, are complete microbiota overhauls needed via fecal transplant procedures, as we've heard of in the media?

It's tempting to rely on modern medicine to provide ways to directly introduce good microbes to the lower bowels, but removing foods that feed our imbalances is more important than interventions to deliver good microbes. Although the science is complex and laboratory research is ongoing, the solutions still need to focus on what we can do in the kitchen. The digestive system will right itself if allowed to do so, or, if very compromised, with some skillful nudging through herbs, probiotics, etc. As powerful and valued as medical intervention is, there's a secret among clinicians of all types that about half the patients who arrive sick will get better without any medical treatment whatsoever, and half of the rest will get better if they can do the simple but personally challenging thing of removing what is keeping their ailment in place. In Chinese medicine, this aspect of the healing work is called *lifestyle cultivation*, including diet, sleep, fresh air, good water, exercise, and managing emotions. In today's world, lifestyle cultivation also includes mastering computer and television exposure (instead of letting it master you) and managing exposure to news and politics.

Managing our Microbiota with Medical Intervention Alone May Be Difficult

Managing a complex ecosystem such as the microbiota by medical intervention is nearly impossible. As smart as we are, successfully managing nature is beyond our rational or scientific capacity. As an example, the introduction of cane toads to Australia was intended to manage the cane beetle that was damaging sugarcane crops. Cane toads were imported in small numbers to eat the cane beetles, but these toads have no natural predators in Australia. Controlled release failed to contain them, and now there are 200 million cane toads breeding freely there. Toads are great, but these guys grow up to nine inches, weigh a couple pounds, and are deadly to humans and wildlife (even a brief brush on the skin can be fatal).

That was an unsophisticated attempt at ecosystem management. The most sophisticated attempt so far has been the Biosphere 2 closed ecosystem built in Arizona in the 1990s. After state-of-the-art planning, eight scientists committed to living within its sealed boundaries as managers of an intricately designed self-sustaining biosphere. But the ecosystem was not self-sustaining after all. Oxygen levels steadily fell, water gradually became polluted. Although much was learned, life-saving equipment had to be brought in unexpectedly.

Attempting to control complex living systems is likely to have unforeseen consequences. It's better to aim to restore conditions that will allow living systems to balance themselves. The three keys for balancing our own gut ecosystem are:

> » *Reduce or eliminate refined sugar* and refined carbohydrates that allow bad bacteria and yeasts to colonize too high in the intestines.

> » *Eat real foods* rather than processed or over-prepared foods. Rotate foods. Eat at least some whole or unrefined foods. Eat more green vegetables. Eat the peels on organic foods like sweet potatoes or carrots.

> » *Avoid drugs* that kill good microbes, including antibiotics (if possible), NSAIDs, and unintentional chemicals from pesticides, herbicides and preservatives.

Here, it may be useful to review what we know of healthy gut bacteria:

> » There are some microbes in the upper and middle small intestine, but populations are dramatically greater in the ileum and even higher in the large intestine, increasing in population density (and presumably function) further along.

> » Intestinal bacteria contribute nutrients by breaking down foods we can't otherwise digest, releasing nutrients we not only can use but need. These bacteria also synthesize proteins and vitamins, which are then absorbed through special features in the lower intestinal walls. It is estimated that 10 percent of modern nutrition is produced by the microbiota, and it's reasonable to presume a higher contribution before processed foods became common.

> » Intestinal bacteria neutralize toxins and biologically active compounds includ-

ing hormones and digestive secretions. Without this activity, our own secretions and metabolic residues would poison us as they are being collected for elimination.

» Intestinal bacteria are essential for training our immune system. The lining of the lower intestines includes elaborate "testing" structures, where immune cells encounter bacteria of all kinds and are schooled in what is to be tolerated and what to be eradicated.

With all this in mind, it's important that some foods must reach the lower intestines without being digested and assimilated. Gradually increase the following to nurture healthy gut microbiota:

» Foods *high in fiber*, such as whole grains, seeds, nuts, beans, coarse vegetables like kale, root vegetables and tubers including taro, burdock, parsnip, rutabaga, yuca, cassava, yam, sweet potato, sunchoke, water chestnut, lotus root, and high-fiber fruits such as apples and coconut.

» *Roughage.* Keep in mind that the rough part of the food is what feeds the microbiota, not the refined or delicate parts. Think of monkeys and how they eat bananas: they eat the whole banana including the peel, providing a field day for their microbiota. In my local healthy supermarket, there are signs identifying "nutrient-dense superfoods", but most customers' dietary problems arise from excess rather than deficiency. Advice to favor nutrient-dense foods misses the point from a microbiota point of view—we should include more food with low nutrient density, as long as it's real food. Trendy high-protein foods and snacks are also overly nutrient-dense. It's a major shift of mindset—deliberately eating foods that naturally include much that we can't directly digest. (Most junk food, by the way, is high in fat and sugar, and therefore in a different sense is extremely nutrient-dense.)

» *Probiotics* are foods that include their own fermentation microbes (natural yogurts, sauerkraut, kimchi, miso, apple cider vinegar, kombucha, and so forth). Select high-quality fermented foods that contain live fermenting microbes. These beneficial microbes are destroyed by boiling (warming is okay, just keep them well under a boil).

» *Prebiotic* is a term applied to fermentable (non-digestible) plant fiber found in certain foods. This is simply another way to talk about including more roughage (grandmothers' term) with the intention of feeding the microbiota of the ileum and large intestine. What your grandmother didn't know was that not only does this fiber aid peristalsis and healthy elimination, this roughage is digested by bacteria and a dime out of a dollar's nutrition is actually manufactured by the microbiotic workforce low in the gut (more, if the gut microbes are strong). Favorites of prebiotic advocates are sunchoke, dandelion greens, chicory root, onions, leeks, and garlic (note however that onions and garlic are easily too warming for the upper digestion, meaning that, on balance, microbe feeding is best provided by other fiber foods).

Start Slowly with Prebiotics!

Start slowly when introducing high-fiber prebiotic foods such as sunchokes. There is nothing toxic in sunchokes (Jerusalem artichokes) that causes bloating or diarrhea, but if you haven't been eating much roughage, your microbe farm won't be ready to digest the special fiber they contain, called inulin. Belly rumbling, bloating, and diarrhea can result. Tune the microbiota by feeding it what it needs—roughage—but start slowly. Stay with the feeding program over time, and prebiotic high-fiber foods such as sunchokes will eventually digest perfectly.

It's not complicated; any and all vegetable food fiber can be beneficial, not only the trendy prebiotics like sunchokes, chicory root, or leeks. Take beans as an example. Some people say they can't digest beans, making jokes about flatulence, or suffering from distention or other digestive pain. Most people who experience discomfort from beans simply won't go near them. In Chinese medicine, we interpret this as digestive weakness (an aspect of *spleen qi insufficiency*) and recommend spices that aid bean digestion such as fennel seed, cumin, oregano and the other spices described above. Some people feel it's a lack of digestive enzymes and take enzymes in pill or liquid form. But maybe the problem with beans is from the imbalance in the microbiota (or these causes together). The microbiome within each one of us is unique; its balance and vitality is an active part of our digestive health. If our microbiome lacks the good microbes that can digest the parts of beans our acids and enzymes leave, naturally we will bloat as the wrong microbes cause fermentation and produce gas. Given some time, the microbes that thrive on digestive bean trash will begin to flourish, beating out yeasts and competitor microbes because the food they need is steadily arriving, in small but increasing amounts. That's the key: sudden increases in roughage will cause mis-digestion, but starting gradually with a fiber food like beans will selectively breed the appropriate microbial cast of characters. Gradually increase portion size to encourage more of the good players in the belly. *Eat for the microbiota you want.*

A brief anecdote. Early in my training, I had a cooking teacher who was generous and skillful. She cooked beautifully in a modern whole food style. One day she changed her vocal tone dramatically and said, "Look, let's peel these broccoli stems! C'mon, admit it, they're absolutely impossible to digest if you don't peel them! I know it's not whole food eating if you discard the peels, but I hate them, I'm not eating them anymore, they are absolutely impossible to digest, they're disgusting!"

The next time I saw her she apologized for the outburst and confessed that her own health had been in crisis for months, although medical tests showed nothing wrong. I had noticed some degree of disconnect between her cooking instruction and her real attitude, and the broccoli stem diatribe broke that tension—now she was authentic and honest. I didn't know at the time, but what was happening for her was that she had been eating more indigestible plant roughage than her lower intestinal microbe farm could successfully process. She was teaching a cooking style that she wasn't eating at home. When she ate the broccoli stems, she was surprising her intestinal microbes, and that's a recipe for distention, bloating, fatigue and misery.

Without clear understanding, it's all too easy to ricochet between good intentions and guilt-laden backlash. This early teacher of mine was smart and determined, so I presume she found a good way to rebuild her digestive strength, but it took me a long time to understand how to assess and guide people through such difficulties. The answer lies in "training" the microbial colonies in our lower bellies. Developing the microbiota is like exercising to stay fit. Getting no exercise is not good, but too much too soon causes stress or even injury. Even yoga classes can cause injuries. The trick with exercise is to find what's safe right now for strength, flexibility, and endurance, then apply reasonable stress-challenges when well rested and emotionally calm.

It's the same for exercising digestion. Too little fiber doesn't feed a healthy microbe farm, but if you add too much suddenly—as in a moment of inspired commitment to a new whole food diet—the microbiota will not be ready, and too many of the wrong players will cause havoc. From a microbiota point of view, there's much to be said in favor of steady diets like those in traditional cultures. Improvements requiring shifts in internal microbial populations are successful when done gradually and maintained with consistency.

In Simple Terms:

» More fiber of all types improves intestinal health and protects from numerous serious illnesses, but go slowly.

» The intestinal microbial community adjusts to diet.. Make dietary shifts to increase fiber of all types (whole grains, coarse vegetables, root vegetables, fruits with peels, nuts, seeds, beans) slowly and consistently.

» Reduce refined foods that feed the wrong bacteria (sugar, baked goods, chocolate, desserts). Junk food and high-cuisine food both can be dramatically lacking in the array of fiber needed. Foods that feed the wrong microbes don't nourish the good microbes. Another way to view this is to avoid a diet over-weighted to quick digestion.

Be aware of when whole or high-fiber foods are *not* appropriate:

» For the very young, elderly, ill, or anytime you are stressed or exhausted, whole foods can be too difficult to digest.

» Digestion should be pampered at such times, for example, with soups, white rice, string beans, and gently cooked fish.

Roughage is sometimes called *prebiotic*, that is, it provides what the good microbes need to eat. Don't worry about which foods are *most* prebiotic. Eat broadly across vegetables, root vegetables, grains, beans, fruits, seeds and nuts.

I had just purchased 8 ounces of organic pine nuts from a highly reputable neighborhood grocery. Two guests were joining us for dinner. (We were having delicata squash with steamed millet, parsley, lentils, sautéed mushrooms, and broccoli rabe.) The pine nuts were to be toasted and sprinkled through the millet-parsley mix that stuffed the squash. Simple to make and good to eat. I smelled the pine nuts, wasn't sure, offered them for testing to my son—owner of a super-sniffer sense of smell—who told me what I had hesitated to admit: the nuts were off. I couldn't include them in our meal. The next day I returned them to the shop for credit and had a friendly-honest chat with the manager.

» Fermented foods with live microbes are called *probiotic*, meaning they supply living microbes to the system. Include fermented foods in your diet, especially after use of antibiotics or to help restore digestion after years of poor diet.

  • Probiotics include yogurt (only if containing live culture), kefir, miso (don't boil), kimchi, sauerkraut, kombucha, natto, etc.

  • Probiotics may or may not survive the trip through stomach acids to reach the lower intestines where they are most needed. To increase success, eat probiotic foods on an empty (resting) stomach or after vegan meals low in protein. The stomach is not always very acidic, despite popular belief. Protein requires highly acidic conditions for digestion—and thus stimulates acid secretion. Living probiotic microbes suffer from the increased stomach acid secreted to digest meat, fish or other concentrated protein. To maximize chances of probiotics reaching the intestines alive, conduct a modified fast: have a probiotic (miso soup, live culture yogurt, or a commercial probiotic) followed by a light vegan meal such as steamed millet with sautéed kale. This could be daily lunch for several weeks, with ordinary meals containing ample protein for breakfast and dinner.

» Earlier, fermented foods were discussed as digestive aids; the fermentation has already done some of the work of digestion (similar to how cooking helps break down bonds within foods that are difficult to digest otherwise). Fermentation also aids (and therefore relaxes) the gallbladder, liver, and upper small intestine. In addition to those important benefits, fermented foods contribute live microbes that— if used steadily—can help recolonize stressed-out, unbalanced gut microflora.

» Steady inclusion of moderate amounts of yogurt, miso, kimchi, sauerkraut, kombucha, or marketed probiotic drinks or pills is better than occasional or binge use. As with physical exercise, too much at first followed by slacking off isn't wise.

Foods That Digest Themselves

The Chinese medicine tradition has a strong focus on foods that "digest themselves". It sounds odd at first, but on second thought it makes perfect sense. Fermented foods are digesting themselves, as are fruits as they ripen. We just leave them alone and self-digestion proceeds. All we do is choose the right time to eat them: after the process has begun, but before there's nothing left for us.

Cooking, in an important sense, speeds this process or enacts it in foods that are very stable (rice and beans, for two examples). Sprouting grains or beans is similar because they are no longer shelf-stable. Once seeds such as grains or beans have sprouted, we must eat them rather quickly or they will spoil. This is another example of "predigestion" that happens outside the body. Anything that shortens or eases the digestive process will be strengthening for our internal digestive organs that otherwise would have to work harder.

Foods that digest themselves have an uplifting quality. They are less grounding, more about lightness and non-attachment. It's an important part of understanding food that can be used for people suffering with weak digestion. It is also a key for diets aimed to further spiritual development, lightening our sense of burden and attachment.

Here's the most important take-away about intestinal bacteria: The gut microbes will adjust to the diet you are eating. The microbiota has been seen to change dramatically with seasonal eating (indicating the time frame is weeks and months, not years). Starving the bad players and boosting the good guys can be as simple as eating a diet of real foods—always fine-tuning for personal health concerns and individual goals.

SIXTEEN

Nursing the Lower Gut: Resolution of Serious Problems and Guidance for Everyone

Understanding the mechanisms of an illness can offer insights useful for making good health even better. This is a central tenet in Chinese dietary medicine. In other words, if a diet can help a person recover from a serious condition in practical ways, aspects of that diet can help healthy people be even more fully healthy. The reader can choose: read here because you or a family member suffer from problems of the lower gut, feel free to skip this section if it is not of concern, or follow the inquiry into more complex problems of the lower intestines to learn more about optimizing good health.

What Are Diverticulosis and Diverticulitis?

In diverticulosis, the walls of the large intestine lose some integrity, allowing bulging and subsequent small pockets to form (called *diverticulum* because bacteria and some waste are *diverted* from their proper course). If these pockets become inflamed or infected, the condition is called *diverticulitis*. This condition can remain hidden or flare up with extreme pain. Standard treatment is strong antibiotics and often hospitalization.

The diverticulum pockets can exist without symptoms for decades. A single causative factor (such as a specific germ) is not known or expected. Risk factors are known, however, and include chronic constipation, obesity, low-fiber diet, and smoking. Smoking—causing a problem of the lower intestines? In Chinese medicine, the lungs and large intestine are seen as intimately connected, often energetically passing pathology from one to the other, depending on which system happens to be stronger in an individual. Since smoking clearly insults the lungs, it is not surprising that smoking is also a known risk factor for serious large intestine problems. More on this in a moment.

Along with the risk factors mentioned above, a diverticulitis attack—with wrenching abdominal pain that brings life to a halt and sends a person to the emergency room—is often precipitated by acute emotional stress. It is common to hear from clients after the attack is over and dietary therapy has begun that the attack happened "all of a sudden, out of nowhere," but the client may have recently added an emotional shock to a long-standing asymptomatic situation of diverticulum. This emotional shock is often at the ancestral (blood relation) level: a loss in the family, the news of a family member having a serious medical diagnosis, or an intense flare-up of a family feud. Like the contributing factors mentioned above, traumatic stress is not the single cause, but it is important to honestly bring emotions to light as part of restoring health deeply enough to avoid relapse.

As with any ailment of the digestive tract, diet may not be solely responsible for the condition arising, but diet is crucial for management and recovery. During a diverticulitis attack, fasting or a liquid-only diet is recommended for the duration of the crisis. Afterward, an interesting balance needs to be found—a person must eventually eat, but diet must not stress the system. Too little food and a patient weakens; too much can trigger another attack. This is an art, and like all arts, sensitivity is key. The cook must respond to tiny signs of progress or distress, finding ways to nourish within very strict constraints. The basic instructions are:

» Return to broths if distress arises.

» Gradually increase soft grains, such as white rice, especially as congee.

» Rely on soups for easy-to-digest nourishment.

» Next to soups, steaming is the best cooking method.

» Add soft-cooked vegetables as strength and appetite improve.

Awareness of personal comfort foods is also very important, although having them in familiar form may have to wait. New comfort foods may need to be discovered.

Chinese medicine, it can hardly be stated often enough, does not use biomedicine diagnostic terminology such as *diverticulitis* or *diabetes*. These conditions have been known, but each person is treated as the unique individual they are. Their conditions are seen entirely within their personal context, and each "condition" is treated as if for the first time—informed by theory, knowledge, and experience, but without preconceptions. The healing path is often filled with surprises. With this understood, my dietary recommendations for people with serious Western-defined conditions described such as diverticulitis, Crohn's disease, or IBS usually include:

» Broth diet. Bone broth (beef bone) is excellent to build blood, and the bone aspect provides very deep, constitutional-level nutrition. The collagen dissolved in the broth is soothing and helps restore integrity of the intestinal walls. Fish bone broth also nourishes the constitutional level and is too often overlooked. Vegetables may be too difficult to digest for those with bowel conditions, but as healing progresses, more vegetables can be included in the broth pot. Vegetarian broths can also be made. Since we need to reach the lower belly and the constitutional level, begin the broth with dried mushrooms and kombu seaweed, adding carrots and string beans after some signs of improvement. I recommend against chicken broth here because it tends to stimulate an immune response and more inflammation. Even after solid foods can be introduced, continue to include broths. A cup of broth can be a meal—all the ingredients have given their essence up to the liquid. But if it is not filling enough, green vegetables and some cooked rice can be added for a soup meal very easily. See recipes for broths in chapter 7 of Book 2.

» Familiar to those who have stayed in or visited hospitals, gelatin is the first solid food many people eat after a liquid-only diet or a fasting period. Well-made bone broths contain so much collagen that they readily gelatinize when cooled. Gelatin is therefore adjacent to broths on a food continuum from liquid to solid foods. For someone whose digestion remains weak for longer periods, foods may be needed in gelatin form. Fruits are standard, but they may not be the best choice. Most fruits are stimulating, and calming is needed here. Instead, add good quality gelatin to vegetable broth. It sets as it cools to make a gelatin meal for this stage. (Keep in mind that gelatin is animal-based, not suitable for vegetarians. *Agar agar* or *kanten flakes* can make a "gelatin" that is vegetable-based. A kanten recipe is on page 157 of Book 2.)

» After broth and gelatin, proceed as if weaning a toddler. The first solid foods should be congee (wet, soft-cooked white rice porridge). In this and other cases of severe digestive distress, plain congee can be very effective. (This therapeutic use marks an exception to the rule that congee is always served with condiments and accompaniments to add nourishment and tune energetics. Here, plain, salted congee can be used.) After plain congee can be well tolerated, continue with congee along with condiments that aid digestion. Examples include slivered fresh ginger and mashed sweet potato or butternut squash. Millet porridge is often the next choice; millet is also very soothing but does include whole grain fiber. Some people, unaccustomed to these healing foods traditions, may object to a diet of broths and congee, but there are times when healing requires this degree of focus and discipline. Acting as the cheerleader for the patient or family member is often very important.

» The next group of foods for supporting recovery from lower bowel illness are the familiar soothing small intestine foods: zucchini, squash, gourds, sweet potato. For patients at this stage, hospitals often advise cooked, peeled fruits and vegetables, even from a can. White bread is also commonly recommended. "Well-cooked and low fiber" is the message, but good quality and better tasting foods can always be a part of a healing diet. I recommend avoiding vegetables from a can and commercial white bread (remember, herbicides such as Roundup turn up in most commercial breads). I recommend staying with congee and millet porridge with soft vegetables like zucchini and sweet potato through this period.

» Cooked fruits are also a standard recommendation at this point, but again I advise reserving fruits for middle or later stages of recovery. Fruits can be too sweet, feeding yeasts and other bad microbes higher in the intestines. Fruits also contain fiber, which can easily be too stimulating at this point in recovery (although beneficial later). Energetically, fruits are the *yang* expression of their plant, their plant's goal. More than merely a sugar boost, fruits carry this *yang* energy. *Yang qi* is a *moving energy* that may cause pain or discomfort if used too soon. Pay close attention to assess if introducing fruits causes pain or diarrhea; adjust accordingly.

» Until fairly recently, medical advice was adamant that patients with diverticulitis must avoid eating seeds, fearing small seeds would get caught in the diverticulum pockets. The seeds implicated included poppy, sesame, and the tiny seeds contained in raspberries, strawberries, figs, tomatoes, cucumbers, and zucchini. The idea was that small bits like sesame seeds might be swallowed whole and resist upper digestion, then lodge in a pocket and decay there rather than either digest or pass. There is no evidence for this idea, however, and current advice neither prohibits nor even discourages eating seeds. Seeds that have specific resonance with the small and large intestines can be of great benefit. Start with chia, a very soothing and gelatinous seed. Zucchini and okra are also gelatinous and can be used here with good results. Eggplant is a densely seeded gourd that has direct connection to the large intestine; although it is a nightshade and problematic for some people, eggplant can be used therapeutically at this point to stimulate movement and clear inflammation. Most seeds resonate with the lower belly center. Because they have oils to moisten the intestines and have some degree of descending/downbearing energy, they will also energize the large intestine. Seen this way, it's possible to understand why eating seeds too soon may cause discomfort, yet be helpful later (and why seeds initially raised a flag of alarm for Western clinicians treating those with diverticulitis). It wasn't a problem of seeds decaying in the diverticulum, it was simply that the energetics of the seeds were stimulating the large intestine too much, too soon. Seeds are fine after the initial two healing stages of broths and congee.

» As healing continues, focus turns to health maintenance and prevention of recurrence. Constipation is to be avoided. A diet rich in fiber of various types promotes peristalsis and supports healthy microbial colonization (and thus good large intestine health). Now, other seeds can be added such as flax, hemp, or tiger nuts (another prebiotic, tiger nuts are a very small tuber currently being marketed as a snack "nut"). Rather than continuing a refined food diet with added fiber supplements, gradually convert to a balanced diet with mixed grains, wide variety of vegetables, root vegetables, cooked fruit with warming spices such as cinnamon, ginger, scallion, nutmeg, turmeric, rosemary, oregano, cumin, cardamom, coriander and so forth. Seaweeds, incidentally, are moistening, soothing, and clearing, perfect for the large intestine. Gradually build up to full fiber eating. Fiber in the gut is soft, it's not scratchy as many imagine. The discomfort some people feel from fiber—remember my early cooking teacher who couldn't eat broccoli stems—is not from physical irritation of the lower intestine, but from the lack of appropriate microflora that would naturally digest it. This is about restoring microbial balance and intestinal integrity slowly and steadily.

As with all healing, what to avoid is often more important than what to add. With a delicate lower intestine, avoid:

» Raw food. Cooking food greatly aids the entire digestive process.

» Cold food. Cold food and drink taxes digestion. While it is true that even cold foods have warmed to body temperature by this time, the insult that cold brings can sink to the large intestine (and the lower belly in general). In particular, cold drinks must pass by the lungs, and as mentioned above, the lungs and large intestine share a very close connection, being considered a *yin-yang* pair in the classical organ system (theoretical, yes, but often demonstrated in the clinic). The lungs do not like cold; cold air or cold drinks often stimulate a shallow protective cough, as the lungs attempt to push out the offending cold. In the case of iced drinks, the cough doesn't work, we proceed to swallow the cold drink and then sip more. This damages the *lung qi* and this cold damage can transfer to the large intestine.

» Eating ice chips is a standard recommendation for people recovering from diverticulitis, but this is a very poor practice. The cold introduced is significant and should not be discounted. No functions of digestion improve with the introduction of cold, nor are ice or iced drinks beneficial to treat hot conditions or inflammation. Remember, to treat inflammation and problems from heat, we want to reduce causes, clear heat, and nourish fluids. The addition of cold fulfills none of these needed strategies and can add to already complex difficulties.

Large Intestine Health Is for Everyone

Diverticulitis is a severe condition that effects relatively few. I'm including it here in some detail as an overview of a dietary strategy for healing the large intestine from severe distress. The principles used for healing this type of problem can be used by everyone to maintain and optimize good health:

» Feed all the areas of your digestion, from appetite to the microbe farm of the lower gut.

» Include a good mix of whole foods including natural fiber (vegetables, grains, nuts, seeds, fruits, tubers, sea vegetables).

» Processed foods, packaged foods, fast food, and gourmet high cuisine foods usually lack sufficient and varied fiber.

» Fiber is good, but there are times when low-fiber foods are important, for example, when very young, when elderly, when exhausted, or when ill. White rice, for example, lacks fiber and many nutrients included in whole rice, but it is very useful for soothing digestion and nourishing *yin*. It's an art; the best diet is personal and ever-evolving. Avoid dogmatic ideas of good or bad, stay open-minded about food choices.

» Vegetables, fruits, and spices add directionality, needed by everyone most of the time.

» Good breathing connects to the large intestine through its relationship with the lungs. The *qi* for elimination comes from the lungs; weakness in the lungs will make elimination very difficult. To understand this for yourself, ask someone who recently fractured a rib and can neither breathe freely nor apply any breath effort when eliminating. They will tell you how important lung function is for moving the bowels. This helps us understand the mechanical contribution of the lungs and chest for elimination, but descending *lung qi* is providing directional energy for peristalsis all along, hidden from awareness in the complexities of the enteric nervous system. In the clinic it is clear that when *lung qi* noticeably lacks descension, the passage of food through intestines is slowed and elimination regularity is disrupted. (The relative strength and directionality of *lung qi* can be clearly sensed through the Chinese medicine art of pulse reading. For those not trained in reading pulses, much information on the status of *lung qi* can be gathered by listening to the quality of a person's voice and by observing the specific qualities of their breathing.)

» Foods should be cooked, and cold drinks generally avoided. It's better to avoid raw food and cold drinks, which can have the effect of driving inflammation deeper into the body. It's important to treat heat or inflammation skillfully rather than attempt to subdue it with cold drinks.

» Inclusion of probiotics (foods containing live beneficial microbes) and prebiotics (foods that deliberately feed the helpful microbes with ample and varied fiber) can be useful, but specially packaged pre- and probiotics are not necessary. Fermented foods provide healthy microbes (and other benefits) and the prebiotic function of sufficient fiber is naturally included in a varied diet that is not too fancy or too junky.

Continuing Further: The Problem of Hemorrhoids

While diverticular disease is relatively rare, hemorrhoids are unfortunately common. Chinese medicine differentiates several types: internal, protruding, bleeding, and so forth. What is most important to know is that hemorrhoids occur because diet and lifestyle have caused two general types of failure:

» Sinking of what needs to energetically ascend

» Reduced integrity of blood vessels walls (hemorrhoids are a type of varicose vein)

To reverse the problem, diet should support the uplifting aspect of digestion, or in the more specific terms of Chinese medicine, the ascending quality of *pancreas-spleen yang qi*. The importance of pancreas-spleen *yang qi* being supported in turn by *kidney yang qi* was described in chapter 12.

Foods to support *pancreas-spleen qi* ascension include:

» Non-glutinous grains (especially if soaked prior to steaming)

» Ascending vegetables such as asparagus or celery

» Spices (definitely not the hot spices, but the warming kitchen herbs and spices: rosemary, oregano, dill seed, cumin, caraway, cardamom, coriander, mustard seed, nutmeg, cinnamon, clove, ginger, turmeric, scallion, and with some limitations, garlic)

The second aspect here—integrity of the blood vessel walls—can be supported by the inclusion of buckwheat (kasha) in the diet, as well as certain fruits best consumed warmed: apricots, prunes, figs, raisins (or grapes), citrus peel, and cherries (a template recipe for stewed fruit with warming spices is on page 163 in Book 2).

To someone suffering annoying (or acutely painful) hemorrhoids, this dietary approach may not seem like strong medicine. Symptom relief is important, but symptoms recur until causes are addressed, and the underlying cause is failure of *pancreas-spleen qi* to ascend and uphold as it should. The reasons for this need to be sorted out as well—is it purely dietary, or does adrenal exhaustion underlie *pancreas-spleen qi* sinking? Perhaps constant worry is sabotaging digestion. Has the pancreas-spleen been burnt out by overeating sweet foods and refined grains (cookies, sweet baked goods, candies, noodles, white breads, sweet snacks, sweet drinks), or has it been overwhelmed by liver stress from too much fried food and excess alcohol consumption? The liver has connections of *qi* and blood through the groin and anus area, and liver stress can therefore directly (and indirectly through pancreas-spleen) impact the blood vessels that partially fail in cases of hemorrhoids. With all this in mind, cleaning up the diet, stress, sweets, or alcohol habits, and engaging in some healing exercise (such as qigong or yoga) is required to successfully resolve hemorrhoids completely. Here is a step by step:

» Simplify meals (see chapter 9 for how to design clear meals to improve digestion).

» Avoid overeating (food stagnation leads to constipation which leads to straining to eliminate).

» Follow steps to normalize the stool: white rice for loose stool, whole grains for constipation, more vegetables for directionality (any directionality will help avoid food stagnation), beans with the spices that aid their digestion, nuts and seeds to provide descension and moisten the intestines, and importantly, morning water. Be sure to drink additional water through the day and plenty of hydrating porridges, soups and stews.

» Avoid intemperance with alcohol. To heal hemorrhoids, have no alcohol for several weeks to permit healing and explore what role alcohol is playing in the condition for you.

» Increase fiber consumption gradually, along a wide range of fiber types:

  ◆ Green vegetables (broccoli, kale, cabbage, Brussels sprouts, string beans, etc.)

  ◆ Rotating grains (white rice, brown rice, black rice, millet, buckwheat, oats, corn, quinoa, amaranth, teff, barley, wild rice). Barley contains some gluten, but it is also very soothing to the intestines. Barley also drains dampness (swelling and water retention), an important aspect here. Soaking grains overnight helps with digestion; even an hour of soaking makes grains noticeably more delicious and digestion-friendly. Dry-roasting grains adds warming and uplifting *yang qi* to help reverse the collapse of ascending energy that underlies hemorrhoid development. Grains (as well as seeds and nuts) can be soaked and then dry-roasted to gain both types of benefit.

  ◆ Small beans (remember, large beans are more difficult to digest). Begin with bean sprouts. Mung and lentils sprout at home in a day or two. Beans just beginning to sprout should be cooked until soft; fully emerged bean sprouts need only to be warmed for 2 to 5 minutes prior to serving. Adzuki beans also sprout easily at home (and are available commercially germinated as well). Have small beans that have not been sprouted as well. My preferred beans here are black lentils, mung, adzuki, black beans and black-eyed peas. Sometimes black soybeans are available; they are traditionally classified with an important kidney affinity and are excellent for any issues of the lower burner, including hemorrhoids. It is acceptable to buy the larger beans precooked in cans, or you can soak your own overnight to cook the next day. Lentils and mung beans cook so quickly that the canned option is hardly an advantage.

- Cooked root vegetables: carrots, beets, sweet potatoes, turnip, parsnip, daikon, yuca, leek. Three delicious and very helpful root vegetables that are often overlooked are celery root (celeriac), rutabaga, and parsley root. These vegetables have a particularly strong benefit.

- Seeds provide fiber, important oils to moisten and lubricate the intestines, and descending energy to aid peristalsis. The three seeds most often used are chia, hemp, and flax. Chia pudding can be a stand-alone snack, or breakfast. Use coconut or nut-milk in place of dairy if any digestive disorder is present (a Chia Pudding recipe is on page 152 of Book 2). Flax and hemp seeds should be cracked or ground before being mixed with other foods, since they won't be of much benefit if swallowed whole.

Fruits also contain important fiber, but:

» Modern fruits are bred for maximum sweetness and therefore can easily support the wrong types of internal microbes. Care must be taken; eat fruits in careful moderation if digestion is not right.

» Unripe fruits are problematic for some people with hemorrhoids. While unripe fruits stimulate the liver and especially gallbladder—and therefore have important uses for those organs—they are difficult to digest and specifically irritate hemorrhoids. Bananas, in particular, are harder to digest when their skins are still yellow; for best digestion bananas should be eaten well-speckled or even past that. Less-than-ripe fruits can be cooked. Most stores sell unripe fruit for appearance and shelf-life, and while chefs may grill a peach or other fruit, they typically select unripe fruits that will remain firm when grilled. Here it's better to steam fruits for about five minutes, or stew mixed dried fruits in red wine and apple cider vinegar with warming spices such as cinnamon, nutmeg, clove, star anise, and vanilla. At the very least, pay attention to your own experience with fruits, ripeness, and hemorrhoids, adjusting accordingly.

» As mentioned on page 154 of this volume, figs and prunes have a special connection with the large intestine, stimulating peristalsis and aiding elimination. Prunes are dried plums of a slender Italian variety, so by extension we can include all plums, and even other stone fruits such as apricot. Although prunes (and prune juice) are the go-to laxative fruit for many, figs can be even better, especially long-term. (Yes, prunes and figs can be used together or in alternation.)

» Since the lungs and large intestine are energetically connected, the lung fruits can also be included here: apples, pears, and Asian pears. Their moistening and descending energy will aid elimination while hemorrhoids are healing. Again, baking or poaching with cinnamon and other spices will provide their benefits without introducing unwanted cold from raw or slightly unripe fruits. Applesauce is easy to make and is much better than raw apples in this context.

» Almond is a nut that strengthens lung function and also moistens the intestines. A great snack to heal or prevent hemorrhoids is a homemade trail mix of almonds, dried figs, dried apple, and flaked coconut (a large intestine starchy fruit, or prebiotic in another way of thinking). Dried fruits are less cold than fresh, raw fruit.

» Other fruits to think about in this context are quince and the special dried sour plums used in Chinese herbal medicine called *wu mei*, or mume in English (pronounced *moo-may*). For those unfamiliar, a quince look like a bright yellow pear (it is a close botanical relative of pears and apples). Available fresh only briefly during the harvest season, quinces taste sweet and tart. The rest of the year quince is available preserved as a thick paste, or in a jam used as a condiment. In contrast to the sweet-tart quince, *wu mei* plums are too sour for most people to eat even when ripe. They are often used to make a digestive tea to stop diarrhea. *Wu mei* plums are also picked green, before ripening, then brined with salt and purple shiso leaf. This salted version is widely available as *umeboshi* plum, a strong digestive aid for the stomach and upper intestines. *Umeboshi* plums are available whole or as a paste (eat one plum or 1/2 teaspoon paste to settle digestion).

» Spices are important, but remember to distinguish between hot and warming spices. Avoid hot spices but do include warming spices that specifically help the *moving qi* of the lungs and intestines (rosemary, oregano, bay leaf, cumin, fresh ginger, turmeric, cinnamon, star anise, and if well used, mustard seed).

» Avoid dietary irritants, often including garlic, onion, hot peppers, bell peppers, tomato, and any personal allergens or sensitivities (try two weeks utterly gluten-free, for example, as a diagnostic experiment).

» Avoid sugar, avoid chocolate (another common irritant). It must be understood that a bit of sugar can be tolerated by someone with stronger digestion, but if hemorrhoids or other problems have arisen, digestion is by definition not strong. With weak digestion, a good meal can be ruined by a surprisingly small amount of sugar. The pancreas-spleen, stomach, small intestine, liver and gallbladder are all busy digesting the meal in an impressive choreography of movements and secretions, but when a bit of dessert comes in, it all stops. "Why should we work so hard to digest this stuff when this sugar can go right into the bloodstream, and it's blood sugar that we want anyway?!" Digestion halts, blood sugar is elevated, and the brain feels relaxed. But, the digestion is stuck with a big meal that begins to ferment, feeding the bad bacteria and yeast. We soon feel lethargic and look for a place to lie down. Plans to exercise are abandoned. Peristalsis slows, sleep is uneven, and the next day is a bit more of a struggle than the day before, leading to more sweets, more post-sugar crashes, more sluggish digestion, more caffeine, etc., in a self-amplifying cycle. Humans are amazingly resilient; but over time, changes are inevitable, especially if under-rested and over-stressed. If symptoms point to weak *pancreas-spleen qi* or unbalanced *liver* or *gallbladder qi*, surprisingly small amounts of sugar can cause very significant problems. Try two to four weeks with no sugar (including honey, maple syrup, snack bars, fruit). See what life is

Why Are Bananas Bad for Hemorrhoids Unless Very Ripe?

Bananas are part of a very starchy fruit group (think of plantains, a banana type that must be cooked). When unripe, the starches of a common banana require robust gut microbes to digest. If hemorrhoids are present, chances are the microbiota is weak and constipation will result (ripe bananas do not cause constipation, however). Constipation exacerbates hemorrhoids. For best results, eat bananas when they are very ripe. You may want to abstain from bananas altogether if their sugars are too much for your current microbiota, allowing the wrong microbes to flourish.

like when you solve the cycle of poor digestion, fatigue, sugar craving, disruption of digestion, more fatigue, and more sugar craving.

Steps for Liberating Yourself from Sugar

Here is the protocol I ask clients to follow when they are ready to conquer their sugar cravings.

» *First, inspire your intention. Get stoked to get healthy. Plan a period of 2 to 4 weeks as a low to no sugar trial.*

» *Second, cut back to very little sugar.*

» *Third, eliminate sweet breakfasts, sweet snacks, chocolate, snack bars, sweet drinks, and desserts. All sweets. Blood sugar will come from digesting real food. Have grains and eggs for breakfast, real meals for lunch and dinner. Snacks can be carrots, appetizers can be olives. Skip desserts for the trial period.*

» *Look honestly for places sugar is still creeping in.*

» *The first few days can be hard. The rest of the first week can still be hard, but by the end of the second week, you are usually through. Blood sugar is now being extracted from real meals, real food. The change feels amazing. Your trial period of low to no sugar may become your new normal.*

Many people add fiber as supplements to treat the constipation that exacerbates hemorrhoids: psyllium husks or flax seeds, for example, as powder or in pills. Or, laxative herbs are used such as senna leaf (again as pills, powder, or tea). These can be important aids at a point in the process, but keep in mind that:

» Laxatives are easily habit-forming (addictive, actually).

» Adding supplements in order to avoid fundamental change is not a strategy for long-term success.

Different laxatives work in different ways. An experienced clinician can help identify where your problem lies, helping to select the appropriate laxative treatment. I usually recommend starting with psyllium husk powder or senna tea because they are the least habit-forming. Because they work in two different ways, they can be used together if truly necessary. Epsom salt (magnesium sulfate) or Glauber's salt (sodium sulfate) are stronger options, best for dry-type constipation, in simple terms. These can be taken internally but caution should always guide use of strong laxatives. As with any medication, the goal is to get well enough not to need the medication. Elimination is a primary health requirement. If you must choose laxatives, be very careful to avoid addiction. It must also be kept in mind not to expect strong laxatives to establish regularity; after purging the bowels it can take up to three days to form the next stool. For external help toward regularity, bulk laxatives such as psyllium husks are best, but of course, eventually good diet alone is all that is needed.

This Is All Very Interesting, But Do I Really Need to Know This Much About the Large Intestine?

As we have been following the passage of food from appetite to elimination, the discussion has gradually become more involved and complex. Ideas have been introduced and ways of thinking about food developed. Specific foods and related concepts have come around a few times by now. Naturally, the picture becomes more detailed as it is painted.

Nonetheless, a very simple take on the large intestine—and foods that particularly aid in its functions—is well-deserved, especially for those who do not suffer with the problems selected here as examples for how to heal the lower belly.

First, a recap of the foods that specifically benefit the large intestine:

> » Root vegetables and tubers (carrots, daikon, parsnips, rutabaga, turnips, celeriac, parsley root, yuca, cassava, sweet potato, yams).

> » Whole grains, if digestion is strong enough. (Start with millet, oats, and buckwheat, then brown rice.)

> » Beans. (Small beans like lentils, mung beans, adzuki are easier to digest, larger beans are good, too, but only when the microbiota is strong.)

> » Green vegetables.

> » When appropriate, do not peel carrots, daikon, parsnips, parsley root, sweet

potato, yam, soft squashes, etc. The peels contain different fiber types than the inner flesh, often particularly beneficial to the microbiota of the ileum and large intestine. Purchase organic vegetables, wash but do not peel (unless digestion is in distress, as discussed above).

» Ripe fruits. (Some fruits have special resonance with large intestine: fig, prune, quince, apple, pear.)

» Nuts and seeds, especially almonds, flax seeds, chia seeds, hemp seeds, sesame seeds.

» Prebiotics such as sunchokes, dandelion greens, chicory root, leeks, tiger nuts. (These are superstar prebiotics, but all fiber types are helpful.)

» Fermented foods (yogurt, kimchi, sauerkraut, miso, kombucha, and more).

The energetics of the large intestine are also very important:

» The large intestine resonates with and regulates water. If you want to communicate with the large intestine, drinking plain water on an empty stomach is one of the best ways. Have a glass or two of room temperature (or warmer) plain water first thing in the morning—before any food or taste stimulation. This aids large intestine health (and therefore health in general).

» Since the large intestine is at the end of the line, it is subject to everything that happens above: appetite, chewing, ease of swallowing, functions of stomach, pancreas-spleen, liver, gallbladder, and the complex aspects of the small intestine. The large intestine tries to make everything that occurred before all right.

» Along with the ileum (lowest part of small intestine), the large intestine hosts trillions of microbes that live with us symbiotically. We simply cannot live without them. These beneficial microbes digest food roughage that can't be digested by our acids or enzyme secretions. The microbiota synthesizes essential vitamins and proteins that are absorbed through special receptor cells into our blood stream. These healthy microbes digest and offer us the benefits of food stuff that scientists formerly believed contained no human nutrients.

» The micro-farm of the lower intestine trains our immune cells in a carefully controlled environment, and we in turn provide the microbiota with the entirety of their life support.

» The best way to support the right kind of microbes is to gradually increase the foods they need to thrive. We repopulate and manage our micro-farm with our regular diet. The appropriate microbes will select themselves if we eat as recommended here, good being fed and bad being starved off.

» Food cravings need to be acknowledged, understood, and skillfully solved. There is a fascinating theory (supported by ongoing experiments) that the microbes in our gut are actively influencing our brain to provide for their specific needs, usually through strong food cravings. Sugar cravings might be so intense partly because the "bad player" microbes are secreting neurotransmitters that make the brain ache for simple sugar, the food these microbes need to compete with the "good player" microbes. The idea that microbes can influence our behavior may seem far-fetched, but think of an animal infected with rabies—the germ drives the host from the safety of its habitat and compels it to bite, precisely the mechanism needed to ensure survival not of the host, but of the germ. We readily accept that rabid animals lose control of their behavior, so perhaps the idea that microbes in our microbiota compel us to provide their dietary needs is sensible. There is no problem if what the microbiota wants is also good for the rest of our health, but if that's not the case, dietary discipline is required to starve and repopulate the microbiotic army. We need to be in charge of the troops within, rather than letting unruly intestinal microbes dictate our food choices through mysterious and disruptive cravings. When our interests are aligned and digestion is truly working well, the enteric support for clear thinking and fundamental happiness cannot be overstated. A basic list of prebiotics and foods that specifically support health of the large intestine is included above.

» The microbial army in the lower gut is also essential for neutralizing toxins. External toxins include environmental poisons such as farm chemicals or other pollution; internal toxins include strong digestive secretions, hormones that have been collected for excretion after use, and the byproducts of internal fermentation from food that has not been digested efficiently further up the line.

» Don't expect hi-tech solutions to solve mistakes we are making with our daily diet. The microbiota is the focus of an entirely new branch of medicine. Increasingly specific tests for microbiome markers will be coming, much like the DNA and blood tests we've come to take for granted in other branches of medicine. Markers for obesity, diabetes, learning disorders, allergies, depression, and other major concerns have already been identified in the microbiome. This is a stunning shift—this DNA is not "ours", yet it is being shown to nearly control major aspects of our lives. In the excitement, the influence of the microbiota will likely be overstated, and miracle cures will be marketed. If you wish to change the population balances in the microbiota in a sustained way, it is very important that you make fundamental changes in diet, not just adding a special ingredient to fix things while changing as little as possible. Straightforward, strong changes are much better than negotiating with yourself using dietary Band-Aids. No matter how complex the science needed to explain it, simple and sustained changes in diet will make real changes in the microbiota and therefore enable very deep shifts in health.

» Similarly, resist the temptation for one-time fixes. An interesting study of a surviving hunter-gatherer tribe called Hadza from remote parts of Tanzania found that gut microbes change readily with the seasonal shifts in foods. What this means for us is that the microbial balance is something that changes as diet shifts, rather than remaining fixed or permanent. Even if we were able to replace our entire microbiota with a healthier one, if we continue our habitual diet, our old microbial profile will return. We can sustain the microbes we want by steadily feeding them the diet that supports them while avoiding the foods that foster microbial misfits.

» Beyond the microbiota, it is crucial to understand the directionality of foods. The large intestine likes descending foods like carrots and other root vegetables, as well as the bulk provided by earthy foods like grains and sweet potato. If, however, the balancing energetic of ascension (provided by healthy pancreas-spleen *yang qi*) is weak or failing, descension will be too much: problems will develop of prolapse, hemorrhoids, chronic diarrhea, and so forth. In tuning digestion and elimination, harmonizing directionality is crucial.

» Don't rely on diet alone. Exercise is also important for keeping the internal belly fit, but neither the vigorous aerobic exercise or weight training often recommended for cardiovascular health or general fitness. Physical exercise for digestion and elimination is gentle, it's about flexibility of the waist and lower back. Qigong, yoga, or even home-made exercises benefit the intestines if they include squatting, rotating the waist, and gentle forward bending. Combining good diet and insightful exercise is much better than relying on either exercise or diet alone.

Healthy digestion and elimination are intimately connected with emotions. Improving digestion helps emotions and vice versa. It is all completely intertwined. Nonetheless, some differentiations are important. The specific emotions that relate directly to the large intestine are the balancing of holding on and letting go. If we wish to lose some weight, change jobs, move on with relationships, or overcome old wounds, we must explore our habits and capacities regarding holding on and letting go. We must cultivate willingness to change. This is where the popular practice of clearing forgotten possessions from your closet or from underneath your bed shifts from metaphor to health practice: letting go of things we don't need frees us to let go of excess around our waistline (and stagnation within). To cultivate comfort with change, it is often necessary to improve elimination habits. Some sophistication is necessary here. I'm not saying, "It's all in your mind," but I am saying that as we explore foods and their impact on digestion, we need to look at the whole picture, and that includes our emotions. Sometimes this is very difficult, requiring as much bravery as anything else in life.

Even the simple version does not seem very simple. But it can be. Eat well, breathe freely, exercise gently (including bending and turning at the waist), hydrate with food and water, eat real food that includes roughage, feed all the stages of digestion, and become familiar with how physical health and emotions are interdependent.

As I often explain in the clinic, problems arise from causes, and those problems cannot persist if their causes are removed. In other words, when you make real changes in diet and lifestyle, dramatic changes for better health and happiness cannot help but arise. Symptoms often seem to evaporate. When changes don't come, it means either that we haven't done our part deeply enough or that medical intervention is called for. But we shouldn't rely wholly on pills or other treatments. The genuine path to healing begins when we honestly ask ourselves what we are willing to change in order to live free of the problems we have come to know too well.

Ask yourself this question: *Why am I eating foods that I know are keeping me unhappy, or at the very least, keeping me from being healthier?* This may bring up a torrent of resistance. Being able to face your own version of questions like this is sign of being on the path of healing. Integrating emotional honesty with tangible change has a simple and noble name. It's called *doing the work*. It's about embracing change, it's about paying attention, and it's about letting go.

SEVENTEEN

The Cook as Healer

As powerful as diet is, our health is a network of functions, a mysteriously complex system that resists simplification. We must be careful not to fixate on food, or on any single aspect of health. Let me share a brief story. Some years ago, as a very young professional in the music world of New York City, I got to know a wonderful trumpet player named Jimmy who had been working more than fifty years. He identified strongly with his Italian heritage, and we discussed food as much as music (he knew I was studying cooking, qigong, and tai chi, the latter two of which he vaguely disapproved of). We would talk about playing music the way great opera singers sang, then he would say, "Andrew, you have to have your health! A singing sound on your instrument comes from good guts! You know what makes good guts? You have to be able to go to the bathroom like a champion! Nobody wants to talk about it, but I'm a champion. That's the most important thing, if you have that, you'll have nothing to worry about when you're my age!" A few months later, he died from a heart attack in his sleep, after sounding wonderful playing principal trumpet only hours before. I miss him, his laugh and his lyrical sound, but I also learned that no one part of health stands alone as the single key.

Seen fully, the influence of our diet isn't limited to its impact on our digestive health. The properties of foods influence all the organs and all health functions. Heart health, respiratory health, neurological health, muscular fitness and flexibility, learning patterns, emotional health, and everything else. Since food is one of the primary ways we interact with the outside world, diet is also important for our spiritual lives, however we define that to ourselves.

I encourage any reader to treat these books like a favorite restaurant: come back often, have your favorites, but be familiar with the whole menu. Above all, digest well what you have come for.

In Book 2, I offer recipes with cooking instructions connected to the tour of digestion that we have completed. I see recipes as templates for improvisation to be tailored to individual health needs. Therefore, I have kept them very simple. They are teaching recipes, really. They work as written, but once you are fluent with them, these recipes can be adapted for your individual health and tastes. They can become your recipes, part of your personal playbook.

Home Cooks Are Primary Health Providers

The cook who understands food energetics and has a basic overview of health functions is in position to be the single most important provider of health and healing. More than the doctor, more than the herbalist, the cook has a special weapon: in the home kitchen the cook can tune good health by making something delicious. With such power comes great responsibility. After all, it is from loving the wrong foods (or the right foods too much) that most problems arise in the first place!

Book 2 of *Welcoming Food* presents recipes for everyday eating from appetizers to desserts. Each recipe is explained for food energetics, with many details on how to understand specific foods and cooking methods beyond what could be included in Book 1. It's a resource you can use for any cooking that you do, with these recipes or your own. The main thing is to put knowledge into practice, to bring all these words and ideas into the physical realm of the kitchen. Now, it's time to speak the language of taste.

Sources and Suggested Reading: Developing a Personal Bookshelf

Diet and dietary practice are included in the *Nei Jing*, the fundamental text of Chinese medicine, a bible of sorts, to which everything written later must reconcile. The text (composed in the third or fourth century BCE) can be obscure and requires careful unfolding by someone trained in its oral tradition. The *Nei Jing* (*Inner Classic*) is in two parts, the *Su Wen* (*Basic Questions*) and the *Ling Shu* (*Spiritual Pivot*).

For those of us who do not speak classical Chinese, it is useful to compare different translations. The academic version by Unschuld and Tessenow is now standard (2011 and 2016, University of California Press). Other translations of the *Nei Jing* that I use (and find richer and even more useful) are by Maoshing Ni (1995, Shambhala press), Ilza Veith (1949, University of California Press), and the quirky-but-beautiful rendering from the China Science and Technology Press (1997, Liansheng Wu and Qi Wu, translators).

Selections of the *Nei Jing* have been published in an engaging literary translation, with commentaries, by Sabine Wilms titled *Humming With Elephants* (2018, Happy Goat Productions).

Sabine Wilms has also translated the *Shen Nong Ben Cao Jing*, a fifth century CE classic text where foods, herbs, and minerals share equal medicinal status. I have mentioned the *Shen Nong* materia medica in Book 2 of *Welcoming Food*. Also published by Happy Goat Productions (2017), this is an elegant translation of a modern ordering of the entries. I love this translation but rearrange the entries for my own use into what I understand to be the original Tao Hong-Jing ordering. That sequence (or close to it) is available in an English translation by Yang Shou-zhong, published by Blue Poppy Press (1998).

Also very important is the *Shang Han Lun*, the classic *Treatise on Cold Damage* written by Zhang Zhong-Jing in the second century CE. A scholarly translation with commentary by Wiseman, Mitchell and Ye is available from Paradigm Publishing (1998). Although this is said to be the classical text most frequently commented upon by later authors, its main message on the way illnesses (including the common cold) take hold and progress through specific stages has yet to be simply explained in a way that is accessible to the general public. The *Shang Han Lun* inspires a religious-style allegiance among some modern scholar-practitioners, including what can appear to be a defensive protectiveness. This is understandable due to its importance and internal complexities, but I look forward to an open-hearted publication that presents the essence of these beautiful ideas (without being simplistic) for everyone. The *Shang Han Lun* informs various sections of *Welcoming Food*.

The history of food classification within Chinese medicine is long and complex. Some key texts have been lost or burned, to be referred to in later books only in fragments. Many existing texts have never been translated, and perspectives within Chinese medicine have evolved as new ideas emerged and were integrated into the tradition. Luckily, a Ming Dynasty scholar named Li Shi-Zhen (1518-1593) spent 27 years writing a massive and definitive *Compendium of Materia Medica* (*Ben Cao Gang Mu*) in which he collected, compiled, and corrected over 800 previous texts. Li Shi-Zhen's *Compendium* remains the standard for food (and herb) classifications within the Chinese medical tradition. A complete translation is available from the Foreign Language Press in Beijing (2012). I use an eight-volume condensed version from the same publisher to support the extensive oral teachings on this and other texts I have been fortunate enough to receive.

A number of modern books extract and transmit Li Shi-Zhen's teachings that are specific to foods. I like Ute Engelhardt's *Chinesische Diatetik* (in German, several volumes, 2006, Urban & Fischer, Munich). Another, in English, is *Your Guide to Healing with Foods & Herbs* by Zhang Yifang and Yao Yingzhi (2012, Shanghai Press). Henry C. Lu's *Chinese System of Food Cures* (1986, Sterling Press) also extracts Li Shi-Zhen's food information from the *Compendium* for modern readers. Herbalists can find many food entries based on Li Shi-Zhen's collection in the standard modern English *Materia Medica* of Bensky and Gamble (1993, Eastland Press, 4 pounds 2 ounces). Livia Kohn's *Daoist Dietetics* reviews the more esoteric use of food in the monastic and solo hermit traditions (2010, Three Pines Press).

Tibetan Medicine is another tradition that can contribute deeply to the modern world, and while it is not my principal focus for dietary healing, it is an influence that I welcome. Chögyal Namkhai Norbu has written on health and diet as a small part of his enormous overall output. Two books that may be of interest are *Healing With Fire* and *Birth, Life, and Death*, both published in English by the Italian press Instituto Shang Shung (2011, 2008).

Home fermentation is a growing movement with much to offer, once the energetics of fermentation are understood. One book with instruction and cultural history is *Fermentation & Home Brewing* by Jessica Childs & Eric Childs (2016, Sterling Epicure press).

Giula Enders' *Gut: the Inside Story of Our Body's Most Underrated Organ* is a useful and entertaining guide to the revolution currently underway in the scientific understanding of the microbiota. Written while still in medical school, the author refers almost longingly to the contributions Chinese medicine can make to actually manage what she is describing, but her book focuses on biomedicine research in plain language (2015, Greystone Books).

Hydration is perhaps the single most misunderstood health fundamental. While I have tried to emphasize in *Welcoming Food* the importance of wet-cooked food for better assimilation of fluids, the case for water per se is made very well by the charming and accessible *Your Body's Many Cries for Water: You're Not Sick, You're Thirsty*, written by F. Batmanghelidj, M.D. (2008, Global Health Solutions).

I love reading about the history of food and cooking. *The Lost Art of Real Cooking* by authors Ken Albala and Rosanna Nafziger is a delightful collection of cooking instructions from just before the modern era (2010 TarcherPerigee).

As a cook, gardener, writer, and teacher, I love the little book by Aliza Green, *Field Guide to Herbs & Spices* (2006, Quirk Books). It's an excellent reference that can fairly easily be integrated into a food energetics perspective.

Harold McGee's definitive *On Food and Cooking: The Science and Lore of the Kitchen* (2004, Scribner) is a beautiful book. His focus on science belies a cook's heart, and while food energetics is outside of the author's stated interest, I love this masterful book on kitchen science.

For Western medical information I very much like a study text first given to me by an emergency room physician friend to support my integration of classical and modern health practice, *The Color Atlas of Physiology* by Stefan Silbernagl and Agamemnon Despopoulos (updated 2015, Thieme).

While the internet can be notoriously unreliable, for consensus information on biomedical nutrition research I have referred to the websites of the USDA National Agriculture Library, the Mayo Clinic, NIH, FDA, and various others.

Acknowledgments

One night, while working to complete this book, I had a vivid and powerful dream. In the dream, I walked into a grand building and noticed that my key teacher, master-physician Jeffrey Yuen, was preparing a huge banquet. Although there were others present who seemed ready to help, Jeffrey was in front, handling everything that needed to be done. He was unassuming, smiling, enjoying himself, and doing what a hundred people together couldn't do. I woke with a familiar and overwhelming sense of gratitude. This is what Jeffrey does for us—he provides an unequalled banquet of the stunning and humbling lineage of Chinese medicine. The banquet is the transmission, and there is something for everyone. It is up to us to use it well. I am forever thankful to **Jeffrey Yuen** not only for his enormous generosity and unparalleled mastery but for his encouragement to me to make the teachings my own and to be creative in application of time-tested knowledge and methods.

I am grateful to my many dietary clients and students whose progress has been an inspiration and whose questions have pointed the way to what's needed first.

My thanks to the amazing team at **Classical Wellness Press** to bring this book into form.

Kate Whouley's editing skills and deep engagement with the project have been absolutely invaluable.

Richie Vitale offered his eagle eye to copy editing, earning the Chinese medicine nickname, Riqi.

Dorian Hastings is a proof-reader par excellence, an author's comfort in ways that exceed her job description.

Cody Dodo brought his expertise in Chinese medicine and book design together (again) and has my deepest appreciation.

I sincerely thank the following:

Chögyal Namkhai Norbu (1938-2018), the eminent Dzogchen master with whom I studied for twenty years, whose many turning words have clearly marked "before and after" moments in my life and work.

Philip Glass, who not only read and meticulously marked an early draft of this book but invited me nearly thirty years ago to perform in the Philip Glass Ensemble (and thus eat extensively) across Europe, North, South and Central America, Asia and Australia.

Anne Marie Colbin, with whom I trained in differing dietary theories and health-supportive private-chef cooking skills.

Margie Joy Walden, who opened the first doorway to personal healing for me with kindness and wisdom.

My heartfelt gratitude includes many who read early sections or full drafts and pointed the way to clarifications and refinements.

Betsy Sterman not only read and marked an early draft with her author's instinct but taught me from childhood the importance of home cooking.

Susan Proctor read and improved a key chapter with her eye for detail and style.

Evan Rabinowitz generously shared his classroom and students as this material was taking form (and Diane and Noah as well for the countless meals and conversations shared).

Many others have contributed in different but important ways to this work: **Linda Puckette, Brian Cullman, Margaret Steele, Gabrielle Zlotnik, Tanya Reydel, Monica Martin Prats, Teresa Thompson, Lisa Bleasdale.**

Ravi Sterman took the cover photographs with his ever-growing skill.

Miriam Sterman read sections of an early draft when she was 10, encouraging me with the most beautiful appraisal, "Dad, you say this is a food book, but it reads like a real book, I can't wait to turn the page and see what comes next!"

Ann Cecil-Sterman, my partner in love and learning, contributes an immeasurable amount to my work, from inspiration to fruition. Her knowledge of Chinese medicine is precise and profound, and it is to her that I turn first and last for discussions of the nuances of theory and practice.

Index

About the Cover

One morning I quickly tapped out some grains and small legumes into a pattern on our dining table, as monks do to create sand mandalas. My son Ravi photographed the result, and then we did another. I liked it, and with the encouragement of artist and design friends, we decided to use this personal art for the two covers of *Welcoming Food* (Cody Dodo did his magic turning the photographs into design). The evening after arranging these "grain paintings" we hosted a dinner of practitioners who had gathered in New York from many parts of the world. I cooked the cover art as part of our dinner—nothing wasted.

About the Author

Andrew Sterman's dietary work integrates Chinese medicine with modern cooking. He teaches cooking for health in classes and private sessions throughout North America, Europe and Australia, and his articles and online *Food Chats* have introduced classical food energetics to a widening circle of health professionals and food lovers.

As a musician and composer heard on film scores, recordings, live theater and concert stages around the world, Andrew has had unique opportunities to learn from chefs and family cooks of many cultures. This integration of traditional food wisdom collected from decades of traveling informs his special way of incorporating food and healing into daily cooking routines. Andrew lives in Manhattan with his wife, acupuncturist and author Ann Cecil-Sterman, and their two children.

CPSIA information can be obtained
at www.ICGtesting.com
Printed in the USA
BVHW050012121220
595386BV00002B/51

9 780983 772209